SPLIT LIPS

Stories About Love & Sex

COVER ART:

APOLLONIA SAINTCLAIR

EXTERIOR DESIGN:

BRADEN WISE

INTERIOR DESIGN:

CHAD FJERSTAD

PUBLISHED BY:

EPHEMEROL
= NIGHT =
TERRORS

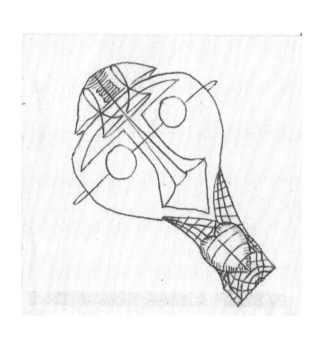

"You haven't been in love,
if you haven't let it ruin your life..."

*- **Sarah Hildebrand***

FAILED FETISH

by Niko Sonnberger

My first time was with a fork. I know: such a cliche. I spent an hour nervously scanning the silverware with my finger tips. What tool will feel the best? The fork seemed obvious, the two-prong skewer was more anatomically conducive, and the butter knife seemed desperate. I wet my hands, picked up the fork and slid it in the electrical outlet with ease. I had never had 110 volts run through my body before, everything was light. My eyes rolled into the back of my head like cherries in a slot machine. Bingo. I was hooked.

As a novice, there was nothing refined about tastes. I had no hard limits, all electrocution was welcome. Fortunately, the human body is a wet sack of conductivity and I was a neon saint ready to absorb the blood of machines. Signs warning "high voltage" were my exponent of breath. It was like edging, but with death. As my love grew like a mold, the crystals in my head held each spark.

The first sunset I saw was a migraine. My mother held me in her lightning bolt arms. The glowing ball in the horizon of my skull ached brightly. Anointing my voltaic devils, it all began as a small prod: the first sensation. During childhood, my wool sweater collection grew exponentially when I detected static biting my skin. Then, it was the balloon shipwrecked to my hair at the birthday party, the further romancing of electrostatic.

After, the humid August where I stayed in the lake during the lightning storm naked, a virgin electric. Running my hand over a fleece blanket over & over in the dark. The time I tried to keep electric eels as pets. Holding a bouquet of light bulbs. And my first kiss was a zap. The sound of the toaster hitting the bath water between my legs. And the forks, the enormity of utensils, over and over, wrecking my body like a dream. Eventually, casually considering red murder to get the electric chair and quickly realizing I live in the wrong decade. So many times, wetting my fingers, cracking the bulbs like eggs, all the dissected kitchen appliance, the "lost" extension cords, band-aid bound, burned, bruised, AC, DC. Edison, silver, copper, but always galvanized, always wanting more.

It was 7:36pm. Right on time. The sun had just gone down and I pressed my stethoscope against the light pole. Then it came, like the first breath after anesthesia. All the street lights turned on in a simultaneous orchestral hum and suddenly I was the doctor, the conductor; Tesla seeing the very first flicker into the future. The dark also had its rituals, each night I christened myself. I gathered all the tangles of holiday lights, my particular eucharist, coiled them around each limb like a festive mummy, plugged them in, covered myself with a sheet and fell asleep. As a luminous ghost, a BDSM Christmas tree, I knew somewhere inside I was fallibly human, anticipating the failure in my fetish.

What they don't tell you when you get hit by lightning is, if it doesn't kill you, it leaves a fantastically painful, tree-shaped fractal scar on your skin. This is called a Lichtenberg figure or lightning flowers or sometimes electric treeing. How ominous to name something so fatal after delicate flora. I found it rousing this scar shape abided by the language of the universe, the golden ratio. And I never cared for real trees outside of the flesh, but transmission towers, these were my cherished beacons. They were a symbol of humanity's collective ability to streamline lightning bolts into walls & homes. You see, we all fetishize electricity, just in different forms. Yours may be just a glowing screen, but we are not so different.

I guess this is the part I should mention I am dead. "After all that?!", you ask. Yes. All it took was one bad apple. In my case, forgetting everything in Europe runs on 220 volts instead of the standard American 110. The Europeans have always been extra. And there are only so many glasses of champagne, french clawfoot tubs, bubble baths with several toasters and Edith Piaf blaring until the human body simply fails you. Ashes to ashes, dust to toast. When you die, you return to the first source. And there you are free of your phantoms, tinctures, ceremonies and infatuations. This is where, for first time, the communion of light and dark bent and I saw backwards into my skull. I am the light.

LOVE HOTEL HILL

by Kris Kidd

for Nakid Magazine

"He's snoring. So, I mean, I'm pretty sure he's still alive…" I confide, cloistered in my microscopic bathroom. "…but he won't leave! Like, he will NOT wake up!"

On the other end of the line: static. Sam's eyes roll. I can *hear* them.

I step back into my tiny Tokyo model apartment silently. There's a man (mid-to-late twenties, pushing six foot five) sprawled out on my small bed, his tree trunk thighs tangled in my ivory sheets. His gargantuan feet hang lifelessly off the cliffside of my mattress. Everything about the dude is massive, so… he seemed like a good idea at the time.

"SAMUEL!" I snarl into the receiver.

"The casting van's already on its way, babe."

Just beyond the sleeping giant, my miniature balcony juts out over Shibuya Ward like it wants to jump. The streets beneath it are already bustling with quiet morning traffic, a near-soundless stampede of responsible Japanese citizens starting their days— ordering coffee and walking to work and cute stuff like that. I'm guzzling plum wine. I haven't been sleeping much lately.

"I'm aware of that!" I whisper-snap. "I need you to HELP me!"

"What? How? Why can't you just—"

Shit! I hang up before Sam can finish. *So much for that bail out.* Sam's the only other fag I know in Japan this season (my only confidant and my only chance) and now I'm all on my own. I squeeze the plastic shell of my agency-provided flip phone until it cracks. *Here we go!* I tiptoe over to the giant, jostling him gently on the shoulder. Blackbirds nesting in the powerlines outside crow a sad song in unison.

"Heyyy..." I titter tentatively. "It's um… the morning, and I was just wondering if you maybe had a… a job… or something like that… you should be getting to?"

"Iuhmtireeebuuhhurrr!" Giant roars and rolls over.

I rub my temples with my index fingers and scan the room for a focal point to calm me down. My gaze lands on a digital alarm clock. The van will be downstairs in ten minutes. *MUST you keep fucking yourself sideways?* my brain brays. The blackbirds are still squawking their stressful shame symphony, building to a screechy crescendo. I lock my eyes on the ceiling, suck on my teeth, and scream.

"GET! THE FUCK OUT!! OF MY BED!!!"

Winter in Tokyo is whimsical. January racks soft lines of snowfall all over the city. February anticipates scattered rainfall. My two-month contract is both a blur and a breeze. I bounce back and forth between bookings with alarming ease. The Japanese work ethic is so intense that nobody ever realizes I'm hungover, or still drunk. They assume I'm just as tired as they are.

I'm living on the eighth floor of an apartment building on Love Hotel Hill— a bunch of back-alley streets littered with sex shops and lusty pay-by-the-hour lodging. Life here vibrates vacantly. It pulses with passion. Strangers slip in and out of the hotel rooms below in a neon-lit rendezvous rotation at all hours of the night. Sometimes, when I'm chain smoking on the balcony and feeling like shit (which happens more often than I'd like to admit), I let go of a lit cigarette just to see if the ember will outlast the fall.

It rarely does.

My agent calls me into the office on a Wednesday morning for an impromptu meeting, says I'm bloated and urges me to watch what I eat. His English is choppy, but his message is clear. I flash him an enamel-free smile and resign myself to a diet of orange slices and packets of almonds. I purge both food groups fruitfully in that bite-sized bathroom of mine every time I binge.

Weight loss is a game I know how to win.

In the casting van, boys from London and New York talk about electro music and the ¥500 pocket pussies they've all scored from the sex shops. Sam and I sit together in the backseat, hiding from the straightness of it all. We swipe through Tinder on my iPhone and giggle like schoolgirls. *Harmless fun*, I think to myself as I drain my data, searching desperately for callous company.

"You are… how do you say… gay?" A photo assistant asks, but kind of says.

I nod. We've just wrapped a twelve-hour job and now we're sitting across from each other at some ul-tra-luxe sushi situation on Omotesandō street that the crew practically had to drag me to. I'm picking at a slab of raw tuna with a pair of chopsticks, shuffling it around my plate to make it look like I've eaten— an anorexic magic trick. Photo assistant asks if the photographer sitting next to me is "my type," and I pretend not to hear him.

I toss back a glass of sake and promptly pour my-self another. This is considered bad luck, *but so are a lot of things*. I pour another, and another, and then one more for safety. I down those three hastily. Photographer asks pho-to assistant to ask again, so I reach for my cigarettes and excuse myself from the table. Crewmembers remind me that I'm allowed to smoke inside the restaurant. I pretend not to hear them either.

Back on the streets, Tokyo's twinkling like a tan-gle of fairy lights. I'm rifling through my backpack for a lighter. Photographer sneaks up behind me and beats me to the draw. He lights my cigarette with a wink, then rests his hand firmly on the small of my back. *Arigato go-zaimasu,* I thank him quietly, wincing as his insolent grip falls lower… and lower…

"And then he grabbed my ass!" I rasp, recounting the story to Sam as we trudge toward Shibuya crossing. "…like, HARD!"

"Is that really a 'first' for you?" Sam laughs.

I slug him playfully on the shoulder. My backpack clatters on impact. It's bulging with beer cans. I crack one open and link arms with Sam as we teeter into the intersection. Models drink for free in Roppongi, so we're headed that way.

"I mean…" I chug. "It isn't… but, still!"

The model clubs all have funny names like *Lex* and *Jumanji*. We flash our comp cards to the bartenders and the rest is history. Packs of preteen model girls from Moscow and Saint Petersburg clomp around the dance floors in high heels and high ponies—batting their lashes like they've got nothing to live for. They pour one out for their less fortunate looking homies back home whenever the DJ drops a beat.

It's hard to tell Mother Russia's angsty abortions apart. They've all got baby faces, skeleton arms, and the same low alcohol tolerance. Japanese salarymen in expensive suits lounge on the leather of their V.I.P. booths and watch these little rubbernecked cherubs with focus and intent. They wag their tongues like Pavlovian dogs, conditioned to the sound of an out-of-step clomp.

Sad to see, but like I said— the drinks are free.

x   x   x

A Swedish tech employee I matched with on Tinder begins stopping by the apartment on his way to work every morning I don't have an early call time, and though these mornings are few and far between, we slip into a sort of routine. A Spanish exchange student I met on Grindr calls me every night his classes are canceled (which happens relatively often) and demands that I cancel my plans, too, so he can come over and fuck. This becomes a routine of its own. Suddenly, my bedroom is in direct competition with the Love Hotels beneath it for the most foot traffic.

Sometimes, I worry I'm winning.

Every other morning: my cold white sheets and the call of the blackbirds. An orange for breakfast, a trip to the bathroom, and a cigarette on the balcony before work. Every other night: the karaoke bars or the model clubs. A couple beers in the streets, some dizzying drinks on the dance floor, and a blackout before dawn.

"I want your eyes more dead…" an art director declares on set.

He's confident in his English. I'm lying on my back on the cold tile floor of a photo studio in Harajuku, wearing a grotesquely gaudy Gucci getup and trying to get by. The sound system's been blasting the same shitty house mix for the past six hours. My brain is buckling beneath the weight of another worst hangover.

"…and I want your mouth more sexy, more open."

I clench my jaw and stand to my feet.

Sam texts back instantly when I tell him that I've just walked off set (*You did WHAT?!*) and I ignore his message while I scroll through my contact list to find the exchange student. I beg him to meet me on Love Hotel hill within the hour. He responds even faster than Sam did and reminds me that I am never, under ANY circumstances, allowed to text him first.

I shove my phone into my pocket and attempt to choke down a stress-sob. It's caught in my throat like a rogue pill. Fellow passengers on the JR line observe my swallow struggle worriedly as we hurtle toward Shibuya station. When we arrive, it's pissing rain. I don't have an umbrella, so I make a mad dash for the nearest bar.

"You're a cutter." My newest victim notices, wrestling for my wrist.

We've finally fled the bar by the station and made

it back to my building. It's either really late or super early. He's tipsy and talking a bunch. I have to be on set again in an hour or so. We're both soaking wet, staring at a scar so pink and pronounced, Hellen Keller herself could probably find it if she wanted to. *That was ONE time,* my belligerent brain bumbles, remembering a broken beer bottle.

"No I'm not!" I yelp, yanking my arm away.

When the elevator lands on the eighth floor, we exit it sloppily. I sway my histrionic hips in a coercive little circle as I lead my latest lover down the outlandish outdoor hallway. All around us, the city's strobing and stacked. It throbs like a fever dream— electric, abstract. Neon signs blink at us like a museum of magic eyes.

"Clothes." I command once we're safely inside.

He undresses quickly, his silhouette shaky against the hazy glow of the hotels below. Every angle of him seems to have been chiseled by a Greek God— or at the very least, an ugly old Greek artist. *Dreamy,* I drool until I notice his forearms in a flicker of fluorescence. They're utterly wrecked, basically cutting boards. *Oh,* puzzle pieces shift around in my head. *Sucks to suck,* I sort of think before I crash into bed.

"You're breathtaking." He tells me, breathing just fine.

"You have thirty minutes."

x   x   x

February falls on top of me like a cartoon piano. I reek of champagne, come, and CK One. I navigate the narrow aisles of colorless convenience stores— konbinis, the Japanese call them— in the wee hours of morning, clutching cluttered carts. *Soft stuff only! No more almonds,*

10

those hurt! Ooh, Rice cakes! my brain quivers and quakes while I hunt for binge foods. Shop owners stare me down skeptically.

Whenever I stumble into a pocket of available Wi-Fi (usually back at the apartment) my iMessage goes ballistic: A barrage of worried emails from the therapist I'm supposed to be checking in with weekly. An onslaught of selfies from random dudes back in LA and New York—pictures of them holding their dicks and jacking off and stupid shit like that. I have to put my phone on airplane mode just to shut it all out. *What is WRONG with you?* I lock eyes with me in the bathroom mirror.

And then we purge another pack of almonds.

A few drinks deep at another karaoke catastrophe, I trip over the feet of a male model from a different agency, land in his lap. He checks to see if I'm alright (German accent, or maybe just a gnarly chest cold) but he doesn't ask me to move, so I stay there and grind against him lazily while a skinny girl from Stockholm belts out her best attempt at "Zombie" by The Cranberries. Some lyrics are missing, but I can still relate.

I'm too tanked to complain (or even care, really) when the Swedish tech guy fucks me off the edge of my sorry little bed a few hours later. Pain is something I'm rarely sober enough to recognize. The weight of him sends me crashing into a bottle of plum wine. *Oof!* I stay there, counting shards of green glass until he finishes. The plum puddle sinks into the carpet. The tech guy slips back into his work clothes.

A friend from LA calls on FaceTime, and I answer in a skanky stupor. I skip over the carpet stain and out onto the balcony. She glitches in and out of focus, asks how everything's been. It's noon in Los Angeles, but out here the sky's as flat and purple as a week old bruise. Clouds rush across the wound like they've got somewhere else to be.

"It's great!" I chirp excitedly. "I'm working every day and I—"

Then I realize that I'm crying. I try drying my eyes with the backs of my hands, but the tears won't stop falling. *Come on kid, keep it together!* My friend seems concerned. *Kris, holy shit!* I wonder if she regrets calling. *You CAN'T let them see you like this!* I'm shaking so hard now— practically palsying— that my end of the line kind of looks like a found footage horror film.

"Are you okay?"

Another piano falls, but this time it's me— or my lascivious loneliness, or my grab bag of mental instabilities and emotional shortcomings, or whatever.

"No! I... I think I'm exhausted? Or dehydrated... probably? I work all day and I go out every night... and... there are these guys? These... these MEN! They keep coming over! And I... I keep letting them... or Idunno... inviting them, maybe? I don't even LIKE them... I just... I don't think I can be alone right now and I haven't eaten anything... or kept anything down, I guess... in like three weeks and my bedroom is a TOTAL disaster... and... and..."

Every time I feel like I've finished, another admission of defeat slips from my pouty lips like a wave of vomit I've done nothing to induce. Blackbirds gather on their criss-crossed powerlines, shrieking louder and louder as the sun starts to rise. They're taunting me. I'm sure of it.

"Kris, I think you need help."

Back in the apartment, my digital alarm clock begins squealing like a techno banshee. *Fuck's sake!* I'm supposed to shoot a cover this morning. My plans to purge have all flown out the window and taken perch beside the blackbirds. *You did this to yourself,* my brain bitches, *and you did it on purpose.* And I don't even fight it. I know that I deserve this.

"I... I've gotta go."

x   x   x

"It's not that bad." Sam says, but it totally is.

My ass is riddled with black and blue handprints, most of them Spanish. They sting to the touch. I tug the waistband of my jeans up over my razorblade hipbones. I'm pretending to worry about potential nude shoots, but those never really happen in Japan and my contract is up in less than a week... so I'm probably just crying for help.

"They hurt!" I seethe, seeking sympathy.

"Then stop?"

My brain goes all *Good Will Hunting* for a sec, forms a million mathematic equations in search of an explanation or an excuse. The calculations are contrived and confused. They leave me behind with some variables and body count I can't seem (or refuse) to recognize. The numbers lead to nothing and nowhere.

"Okay!" I clap. "So! Do you remember..."

Sam's listening with his eyes closed.

"...how much you hated the word 'no' when you were a kid?"

I can't tell if I'm asking or shouting. Sweet Sam is nodding anyway, up and down like a junkie in paradise. There's a weight in the room now, a remembrance of childhood. It sinks like a stone, or a heart, or my weight on a good day.

"Well, it's like that." I confess. "Except I think I get off on it."

A few stormy nights later, I'm storming down a busy street. Another model-friend is throwing another model-farewell-party at another model-bar. Everyone's saying drunken goodbyes now, partying and prepping to fly back to our respective countries as the season comes to a close. It's been pouring rain and the city is ugly wet, basically bukake'd. I'm swimming through the crossing and my body is moving in that special way where it forgets it's a body— forgets that it means shit.

My broken vessel takes cover beneath the awning of a konbini and attempts to light a cigarette. It fails, checks its phone: Five missed calls from the exchange student and a few voicemails informing me that another one of his classes has been canceled.

I close my eyes, then text my friends to tell them I'm not feeling well, which isn't a total lie. *I am sick!* I dive back into the crossing. *Like, all the time!* Then, I make a beeline back to the apartment, bobbing and weaving between the low tilted umbrellas and glittery plastic raincoats of Japanese passers-by living happier lives.

"You look different." Exchange student sighs.

I want to thank him, but I don't.

Tokyo sobs as I unzip the fly of his jeans, drenching the balcony and all the clothes I hung out to dry on it earlier. Radiant raindrops in the dark. The Love Hotels below glow rainbow bright in the mist like they're all remembering something in unison— a bad dream, maybe. Like they're trying to forget, but the lights are always on.

And then he's somewhere inside of me, each thrust rattling my ribcage like a bottle of pills. I'm somewhere outside of myself, thinking about lust— about my slutty white sheets and all the men who like to hide in them. *Lust is a lobby*, I decide as I drop to my knees. *Everything about it is finite and fleeting,* I outstretch my tongue like I'm trying to catch snowflakes. *No one ever stays*, I swallow, and then I watch him leave.

Locking the door behind him, I light a cigarette. My phone lights up, but I don't check it. The Love Hotels downstairs are still remembering in the rain— their luminous lobbies making room for transient visitors like lungs do for smoke and air. Elevators rising and falling like heavy breath. Fluorescent lights pulsing like arteries.

Strangers make secret love in the bones of them.

SMUT

by Dan Reilly

Remy slumped down in his dead father's office chair, alone for the first time since he'd heard the news. His father was dead, he knew that, but it seemed impossible.

Every square inch of the office was covered in those ridiculous gold statues. Chuck Remington Sr. never seemed to care much about winning them, he just kept them around in case he needed something to throw in a fit of rage. He had always been dramatic that way. But prolific, too. He must have smashed at least a hundred of them over the years, and there were still enough to fill every available surface in his large, bright office overlooking the Cahuenga Pass. Side tables, a coffee table flanked by two love seats, and wall-to-wall bookshelves, all covered. And not a speck of dust on any of them. He never let anyone else clean his office, and Remy never saw his father cleaning, so he must have done it in secret, when he knew no one would disturb him. Dad had a lot of secrets.

"Dad's dead."

He said it out loud, just to see how it felt. It still wasn't real.

Remy was the only person in the building, and the silence made him anxious. He searched his mind for a comforting thought to replace the dread, but he couldn't get his mind off that last conversation he had with the man who gave him everything, (including that stupid fucking made-up name) and took everything from him. They had a fight about the new production schedule, but it was really a fight about Stacey Lynn, and afterwards, Remy swore that he'd never speak to his father again. He didn't think his promise would actually turn out to be true.

His phone buzzed. It was a text from Stacey Lynn.

"You okay? Can I call you?"

The industry's worst-kept-secret was that Remy and Stacey were an item. It wasn't necessarily bad for him to be dating a Remington Studios contract girl, but he didn't like the way it looked. People would think she was only fucking him because he was a producer, and likewise, that he was taking advantage of his power, but that wasn't the case. He wasn't like that, never dated people he met at work, and neither was she. Stacey was smart, savvy, honest, and tough as nails. She didn't do drugs, didn't have kids or a pimp, and most importantly, she made Remy feel safe. And she gave him hope that there was still a place for him in this shitty business. He was in love with her, but he kept it a secret, because he was afraid his father would find out. And of course, he found out. Everything was fucked now, but Remy still wanted her back, even though they hadn't spoken in weeks. He'd get around to returning the text later.

A copy of Adult Video News topped the stack of papers and porn piled on the desk, probably the last thing Chuck ever read. Remy winced at the cover, a picture of the old man and Stacey Lynn posed on a tarmac like Bogart and Bergman at the end of Casablanca. The cover story was about his comeback. Steve Sinclair wrote a big career retrospective piece, including a rare interview with the old man, just a couple weeks ago. It came out yesterday, when he was still alive.

Remy flipped to the center page.

Citizen Stain: Chuck Remington Reflects On A Bittersweet Lifetime of Love, Smut and Success (Then Failure, Then Success Again)

by The Valley's Own Beloved Porn Curator, Historian and Expert, Steven SinClair

Joseph Finn Donovan, born on November 3rd, 1946 , grew up in a trailer behind the Starry Night Motel in Macinaw, TX, which his father built with his own two hands. He never met the man, and little is known about him, besides the fact that he was at least considerate enough to leave some baby batter behind before being shipped off to Europe to fight the Nazis. He lost his right arm and bled out somewhere in France, and his wife, Anna, received a folded flag for his troubles. Anna took over operations at the roach motel of which she was now the sole proprietor, including a thriving prostitution business, of which she was now the sole madame.

When Joseph came of age, he discovered his penis was abnormally large. Like any dutiful swordsman, he learned how to wield his weapon.

Anna popped benzedrine, drank a lot, and had a lot of boyfriends. Joseph, in need of approval from a nurturing female figure, found a comfortable replacement in the hookers who used the motel to conduct their business. And they adored him. Eventually, he learned the business of the flesh, and honed his companionship skills to the point that he could make a decent living charging lonely ladies (and sometimes men) for his time.

A penchant for having sex in public places turned into documenting his exploits on 8mm film, and making a few extra bucks (and some thrills) by selling the reels to local movie houses to play after hours.

In 1968, at the age of 22, he finally fucked a woman he loved, Maryellen Dewitt Sanders, the daughter of a wealthy plastics magnate. And they filmed themselves having sex. A lot. Together, they sold dozens of homemade movies to theater owners, and started a buzz in the world of underground cinema. More people started to attend these after-hours screenings in cities throughout Texas. Money started to pile up. He changed his name legally to Charles Joseph Remington, and Remington Studios was born.

The success of their flagship film series, a pornified Bonnie & Clyde knockoff called "Sex Bandits" propelled them into the national spotlight, delighting not only New York's trench coat crowd, but also the artsy set, intellectuals and hippies.

By 1970, Charles and Maryellen (who was now better known as "Mary More") were the respective king and queen of the underground smut empire they created. They moved to the blossoming San Fernando Valley of Los Angeles, and had their first child.

His birth certificate called him Steven, but everyone else called him "Butch", on account of his being born (without complication, I might add, thanks to a wide and well-conditioned birthing canal) weighing ten pounds and four ounces. By sheer coincidence, he would later measure his penis at exactly ten point four inches. Hence the tattoo emblazoned on his chest in six-inch-high numerals, "10-4". The artist assumed he was a trucker.

In 1972, they accidentally had a second son. Charles Jr., the "runt" of the family, would forever feel inadequate, because he's the only one who didn't get the big-dick gene that seems to run so strongly in the bloodline. He'd grow up being called "Remy" by his classmates.

Remy rolled his eyes at that. The size of his penis was average, and only accounted for a small sliver of his feelings of inadequacy. His decision to perform in a handful of scenes when he first got into the industry was a mistake that always made his stomach drop when he was reminded of it, even all these years later. Back then he was young, and horny, and got swept up in the sexual energy of it all, and performed in enough scenes to know he was no good at it. But he'd done it, and as a result, the size and shape of his penis, the faces he made during sex, and the way he stroked his dick (backhand, lefty) would forever be a matter of public record.

Charles' penis inexplicably stopped working on November 18th, 1978. The same day as the Jonestown Massacre, but presumably unrelated. After that, his life took a horrible turn for the worse.

Mary continued unheeded in her own sexual activities, and was one of the first people in the public eye to contract HIV, and die from AIDS. Charles spent the late seventies and most of the eighties blowing cocaine and drinking, while his heads of production kept the company afloat and covered up the reality of his breakdown, for the sake of keeping face, as well as honoring company interests (not to mention their own).

That was when the bad times started. From the time he was six to the time he was 16, Remy talked to his father maybe a dozen times. One girlfriend or another acted as caretaker to him and his older brother, Butch, but none stayed around long enough to qualify as an actual parent. To Chuck's credit, he was always relatively sober when he spent time with his children, but he was always recovering from a bender, groping and wincing, affecting the thousand-yard-stare of a shellshocked soldier. He had no interest in children, and no idea how to relate to his own.

Remy remembered the time he found a VHS tape while he was rummaging around in his father's closet. He was 11 or 12 at the time. The only label was "XXX 4", written in permanent marker in what he recognized as his father's hand. He had never seen porn before, but had deduced from context clues that his father was involved in making movies about naked people doing things to each other. He wasn't exactly sure what, but he had a feeling that the answer was on that tape.

The forbidden object remained hidden under his bed for a few weeks, until the chance presented itself to watch it without being discovered. He stood in the large foyer and screamed at the top of his lungs, to make sure no one else was in the house, (sometimes it was hard to tell) before he tiptoed into the living room, sat down on the shag carpet, and popped it into the brand new top-loading VCR.

He pushed down the PLAY button, and shuddered nervously as the picture flickered on. His eyes went wide. Nothing could have prepared him for what he saw. He'd barely even seen a naked woman in his life, but now he stared into a larger-than-life closeup of a woman's vagina, shaved, wet, dripping lube and white fluid, with a large, veiny red cock pumping in and out rhythmically, insistently, in the up-and-over position that only exists in porn, never in real life.

He chewed his lip. The woman moaned like she was in pain, but she liked it. Remy was transfixed by the way her sex organs looked. He had always imagined a perfectly flush little slit, like a Barbie doll with a cut, but this was nothing like that. It was like staring into an octopus's mouth. It reminded him of the movie, "Predator". The lips were pink and purple and red. There were folds upon folds like the meat inside a clam. He stared, transfixed, and started to feel himself becoming aroused.

He took his penis out instinctually, wanting to feel what the adults in the movie were feeling. That's when the camera angle reversed; when he realized that he was actually watching a video of his own father having sex. The air went out of his body, and the all the good feelings instantly went bad. He fumbled his penis back into his pants and reached for the STOP button, then realized that the woman looked oddly familiar, too.

Oh, no. Oh, God, no.

His head went numb, and his heart felt like it slid out of chest, into his stomach. Underneath the thick makeup and the feathered hair was his mother. But she looked unreal, more like a doll made up to look like his mother.

It reminded me of the way she looked in her casket.

Remy felt like he was going to pass out. He coughed, gagged, and threw up on the living room floor, turned off the TV, and ran to his bedroom. He didn't come out until the next day. Chuck actually came home that night, but never asked his son about the vomit, or the tape. He knew what happened.

The memory made Remy lightheaded. He skipped ahead

through the rest of the article to the interview.

When Viagra came along, Charles found new meaning in life, cleaned up, and took back control of his company. Today, Remington studios continues to carry the gold standard of the industry, adapting to the times by embracing technological and social change.

Recently, I sat down with The Man Himself, (dressed in his signature velvet tracksuit and post-cataract-surgery shades) to talk about his legacy, the state of the smut business, and his decision to begin performing in movies again at the age of 70, after a nearly 40-year hiatus.

"I used to be somebody. Al Goldstein, Ed Koch and I had a permanent table at Studio 64. Mountains of free cocaine. Free pussy. The mayor of New York sucked my cock! Now, nobody knows who the fuck I am. Nobody cares that I invented porn. There's nothing left to innovate anymore, because I already did everything."

Your son, Remy, took over as Head of Production at Remington a few years ago. How do you think he's done so far?

"Honestly? And I tell him this all the time, it's lazy filmmaking. Everyone's movies look the same, paint by numbers. Five positions, even the order doesn't change. After the oral it's missionary, spoon, doggy, cowgirl, and then a pop shot on the giant fake titties. Unless she has small titties, then he pops on her face. And always with the cutaway. The edit destroys the whole illusion. None of these guys can fuck straight through to the pop anymore, because their cocks are numb from taking hard-on pills every day."

What do you think they should be doing differently?

"Here's what today's directors don't realize: every time you pick up a camera and start it rolling, what you've got is an opportunity to make a statement. That's a great privilege. Not everyone gets a chance to do that in their lives. So when you set up the lights, hire actors, put makeup on them, point a camera at them, you've got to be aware of the statement you're trying to make. If you don't know what it is, you don't deserve to be there. That's why I decided I'm gonna pick up a camera again. And take my cock out again. My generation and the kids today don't have much in common, but maybe I can change that. Sucking and fucking is the only constant in this society. I like to think we have as many similarities as differences. So, in a way, I'm building bridges with my wrinkled old cock."

That wasn't exactly how he put it to Remy when he told him about his decision to perform again. It was the last conversation they ever had.

Remy recoiled at his father's proposition. "That's disgusting, no one wants to see you fuck."

"I know you don't, but don't presume to speak for everyone. Max still fucks in his movies, and he's almost my age."

"Yeah, and it's disgusting. You know what? You have fun, I quit. I'm not gonna have anything to do with this."

Remy got up to leave the room, but only made it about two steps before his father stopped him in his tracks.

"Stacey is going to be my first scene. You're the head of production, so you're gonna produce it."

Somehow, Remy hadn't seen that coming. He turned around slowly.

"No, she is not."

"Listen, you little shit." He got up menacingly from his chair.

"This is still my studio, and she's my contract girl. I bought her, and if I want to fuck her, I'm gonna fuck her. That's how this works."

He flicked the butt of his Black & Mild cigarillo at Remy's chest. It exploded in a burst of red sparks. Remy wanted to punch him. Thinking back, he wished he had. Instead, he turned around, walked out the door, and closed it behind him. Moments later, he heard a thud and the crunch of broken glass. Another award statue bites the dust.

Remy rushed over to Stacey's house to tell her about his father's proposition. He screamed, he raged. He paced back and forth in her kitchen. Like always, she remained calm.

"Please stop worrying. Everything is going to be fine."

"I know. He can't do this. Your contract has a clause that stipulates you can refuse to work with anyone you choose. I know he's not going to like it, but-"

"Oh, cool. So my contract allows me to opt out of being raped? Remind me to thank my lawyer."

Remy's head throbbed. "You're not thinking of going through with this... Right?"

She bit her lip. Remy was on the verge of tears. He wanted her to answer without thinking, to say she loves him, that she would be no part of his father's disgusting plans, or his movies, or his failing studio. That she'd quit and they'd run away to Napa. What a fucking idiot.

"This is my career. It's what I do. You know that."

That was just over a month ago, and things happen quickly in this business. Stacey went through with the scene, she fucked the old man, sucked his cock, swallowed his yellow cum. The movie was rushed through post-production, and the box cover art was currently splattered all over the web and the trade magazines, including the one he currently held in his hands.

He continued reading his father's last published words.

How have you seen the industry change over the years?

"Everything was done for different reasons back then. We were living out a sexual revolution, and we happened to be holding cameras in our hands. Now, all I see is a bunch of kids playing film school. I was there to push boundaries. It was all about the grease and the sweat and the cum. I was making a statement, you see? I wanted to find that line between arousal and disgust. I wanted to grab people by the backs of their fuckin' heads and rub their noses in it. Make 'em smell it. Bad dog! It didn't even look like sex anymore, it was just stupid human tricks. How many cocks can we cram into one girl? And then everyone else started doing it. It was like the space race. Everyone just assumed it would keep getting worse and worse, until - I don't know - people ran out of holes and started fucking each other's eye sockets. But we kept ratcheting it up, ratcheting it up. Double penetration! Triple penetration! Two in her ass, two in her pussy! 100-man gang bang! And then...well then a bunch of people got fuckin' AIDS. All of a sudden, making our little fuck-movies was a matter of life and death...we didn't sign up for that...it just...it wasn't fun anymore."

The man who was known as much for his raging anger as he was for his raging boner suddenly became melancholy:

"I miss my wife. Something broke inside me when she died from that fuckin' monkey disease, and I could never fix it. This whole thing, all of this, it all came from love. My love for Mary. Later it turned into something else, something ugly, but it started with my love for that woman."

Remy put down the magazine and gasped for air. There was a weight on his chest, like a bowling ball. For a moment, he thought he was having a heart attack. He exhaled loudly, and it turned into a moan, and then it felt like the plug was pulled on a bathtub drain, and he wept. He convulsed, and gasped for air. Salty rivers of snot and tears dripped down his dry, cracked lips, and he cried so hard and so loud that he was almost screaming.

He ripped the magazine in half and dropped it on the floor. Then, he picked up one of the awards. He hurled it at a large, wall-mounted TV, and the screen burst, glass exploding everywhere. He picked up another, threw it into the wall, and it disappeared in a hole in the sheetrock. Another. SMASH. Another. CRUNCH. He leveraged his weight against the wall and tipped the desk over. When it fell, it shook the floor.

By the time he was finished, his hands were bloody, and the room was reduced to rubble. He pushed some broken glass out of the way and made enough room to lie down on the floor of his new office.

He curled up in the fetal position and rocked back and forth, crying the desperate, inconsolable tears of a son who'd just lost his father.

THE MOST OBVIOUS STORY IN THE UNIVERSE

by Caroline Bell

Love is a funny thing. It's hilarious actually, if you know how to take a joke.

I was a little girl when I first realized my capacity to burn as rapaciously as I do, and nothing has been able to stop me since, but when I first met you I can't say I was an immediate mess over it or anything.

We met on Facebook. You messaged me and messaged me until finally, maybe out of sheer curiosity, I gave in and invited you to be my date for the evening. You arrived late, disheveled and in the company of several other people. This went strictly against my newly adopted, "I want to be treated like a lady" policy, and so I completely wrote you off. I spent the entire evening talking to someone else who, incidentally, came home with me that evening, and planned on never inviting you to anything again.

I wasn't angry, just unimpressed, and considering your standing in the Hollywood social scene, I think it was enough to drive you a little crazy.

I went to San Francisco the next day to visit a gorgeous man I could never keep myself from. I thought about you not once. I came home and heard from you a few times, but brushed you off because I sincerely didn't care what late night party you were going to, and that's all you seemed to be offering.

Then one night you asked me what I was doing, and just to get you out of my space I explained to you that I didn't really like the lifestyle you had. That I preferred some quiet existence filled with writing, and dogs, and snow to whatever flashing lights and shots of whiskey you were promising. You invited me along anyway, and somehow, despite everything, I decided to go. I was bored in my house, and thinking, if nothing else, I'd get some amazing footage for an art series I was doing.

I got there, camera in hand, still slightly underwhelmed by your personality, a little thrown off by your erratic energy, and texting that beautiful face up in San Francisco the entire time. I didn't care what you were doing, and you noticed.

It's the weirdest thing. You made one comment, and somehow that one comment changed everything. I was standing there texting some other guy who I was convinced I was in love with, and you said, "You're in your own world right now", and laughed. I suddenly snapped out of what I was doing. All my attention went on you. I have no idea why. It doesn't even make that much sense, but we started talking about cameras, and art, and I went and sat by you inside, squeezed into this one chair in the corner for hours just talking, laughing, and having staring contests. I met a bunch of your friends, and they made comments about how it seemed like we had known each other our whole lives. You spent a long time trying to get a good photo of us together.

I still have that photo. I look at it sometimes and wonder how things went so insanely wrong after that. Not right away, but pretty shortly after that.

The next day we texted about traveling together overseas, hoping trains in Germany, and getting drunk with the locals. We were excited, and I felt my walls coming down, if even just a little bit. I was still cautious, but you were so sweet, and I wanted to believe you.

The day after that you woke up thinking of me, and you wanted to see me, so I let you, and we spent the whole night nervously holding hands, and eventually you kissed me, and I came undone. Suddenly I was looking at you like you were magic, and I have no idea how that happened, but I totally do at the same time. You snapped me out of myself, and showed me how you think. It's this completely unique thing, your mind. It moves so fast, beautifully pulsating through story lines and quips, snapping back with silly statements and observations that most of us could only dream of coming up with once or twice in our lives. You do it everyday. It's incredible, and I fell in love with that part of you pretty hard after that. I forgot to text that beautiful face up in San Francisco back, I started going out for flashing lights and shots of whiskey every night, and cared nothing at all for dogs, or snow anymore. Just like that, it happened.

That's where this story ends, unfortunately. Or at least, that's where the part you're all sweet and I want to believe you ends. See, as soon as you became this magical thing in my eyes you stopped trying to convince me you were one. It's as simple as that, really, and it's not a new story. That happens a lot in the world I think. It's too bad though, because I've still got my walls down for you, and I don't think I should. I don't think that love affair I had with your mind, or the way I melted between your body and your sheets was a good idea to begin with. I do think, however, that life is something you have to just let hit you in the face sometimes. That sometimes you have to allow yourself to be broken down, even if it's by someone who's not really nice enough to care what happens when you do. Sometimes you have to get drunk and stumble around like an idiot, and get tattoos at weird hours, and sleep none, and fall a lot, and get quiet and weird, and forget how the hell you were able to attain that indifference you had in the first place. That was good shit, that indifference, and I know very well that's what hooked you to begin with, but it's gone. I can try and fake it, but I look like an idiot. And truth be told, I know you see through just about everything anyway with that mind of yours, so shame on me for even trying.

I still disagree with the life you're living, but I can't help but wish I was in it somehow. I don't know in what capacity or to what ends I want to, but it really doesn't make a difference, cause I'm all exposed now, so I might as well just swim in the damn thing, and write it all down in hopes that I can see it for what it is; The most obvious story line in existence. Boy chases girl, girl resists, boy persists, girl gives in, boy gets over it, girl says, "what the fuck?" and cries. I think Shakespeare came up with that one. It gets repeated a lot, it seems.

That's the funny, hilarious joke about love. I'm banging my head against a wall over it, in case you're wondering, because it's the dumbest thing I ever did to go out with you that night. It's the dumbest thing I ever did to sit next to you in the chair and talk to you about cameras and Germany. I wish I never had. I wish to God I never had.

BABY WITH JEFF KOONS BALLOON DOG

by Christopher Zeischegg

Judy Fiskin, the American artist and professor of photography and media at the California Institute of the Arts, stands on stage, before an auditorium, three-quarters full.

Judy Fiskin: "Madeline, your work has been described as both satire and critique, and yet your most recent interview in Artforum hinted at an unbridled sincerity; a reflection on motherhood and its loss, and the trials of a contemporary marriage. For those of us here, unfamiliar with the events leading up to your installations, Baby with Jeff Koons Balloon Dog and Saint Sebastian, Our Abandoned Child, would you be willing to provide some context? In other words, what was the inspiration for your work with Mr. Alvarez?"

Madeline Hart, the American artist, coughs and speaks into the microphone perched atop her podium.

Madeline Hart: "Please show the first slide."

The projection screen lights up: an image of a woman with child.

Madeline Hart: "You'll see, on the screen, a picture of my friend, Vanessa, and her firstborn, Ambrosia.

Vanessa was like many of my friends, pregnant by her late twenties and transformed into a mother by her early thirties. At the time this picture was taken, I'd say she was interested mostly in the tasks that nurtured and occupied children.

I, on the other hand, enjoyed my time without offspring.

32

Without other people's too.

But I loved my friend and wished the best for her, and felt bad about skipping her baby shower, and for ignoring all requests to spend time with her during the six months after Ambrosia was born.

On month seven, I planned a visit. To make up for my avoidances.

The day before my scheduled visit, I thought about a gift for Vanessa's baby. To make me look less horrible. In my friend's eyes.

I'd been on a Tinder date to the Broad Museum in downtown Los Angeles, and saw a Jeff Koons art book in the gift shop. I thought it would be colorful enough to keep Ambrosia's attention, and a good enough joke for myself. I hoped Vanessa would find it amusing, because Koons had become so renowned and vilified, like an art world Kanye West. Because... I don't know. We'd both attended a Kanye West concert, after he'd come out in support of Donald Trump, and we'd found it funny. Both the music and the fact that we had to hide our attendance from Facebook friends, or else.

I thought the Koons book would be another overpriced experience to laugh at and to hide on a shelf somewhere, behind a Dr. Seuss or Winsor McCay.

Anyway, Vanessa thanked me for the gift and bounced little Ambrosia on her lap, and pointed at pictures of Jeff Koons' Balloon Dog. 'She'd love one of these,' said Vanessa, which seemed to mean that her baby would enjoy playing with a Koons' sculpture.

No laughter. No, um, understanding.

I told her that an orange Balloon Dog had once sold for $58.4 million at auction.

She responded, 'Oh.'

'There are smaller versions,' I said. 'Attached to a plate. They cost about eight thousand dollars a piece.'

Next slide, please."

A picture of Jeff Koons: Balloon Dog (Yellow) – lifted from the MOCA Los Angeles website, without permission – appears on the projection screen.

Madeline Hart: "Vanessa was quiet for a while, and so I assumed that I'd offended her.

'Are they popular with children?' asked Vanessa. 'I'm sorry that I haven't heard of them. I feel so uncultured.'

It was hard to tell whether she was serious. Most likely, we'd both become mean.

I said my goodbyes, because she'd guilted me, and because I knew she'd meant to strike at the way my life had failed most.

In short, I'd tried my hand at writing, photography, and mixed media sculpture. But I only lived above the poverty line because of my father. Without him, my annual income averaged about six hundred dollars.

Vanessa, despite no career of her own, had everything. Because of her husband, Ernst. Because she'd fucked him and given him a child.

I remember what Vanessa said to me as I left her house that afternoon: 'I hope you can afford a dog for your little one some day.'

Next slide, please."

A poster for the film, Nocturnal Animals, starring Amy Adams and Jake Gyllenhaal, appears on the projection screen.

Madeline Hart: "It was maybe six months later that I thought of the Balloon Dogs again.

I was on a Tinder date with Jordan, my husband, who's here with me tonight."

A short round of applause from the audience as Jordan Alvarez, the American artist, approaches the podium.

Jordan Alvarez: "Hello."

Madeline and Jordan take turns with the microphone.

Madeline Hart: "I suggested that Jordan take me to the latest Tom Ford film, Nocturnal Animals.

We sat in the dark and occasionally glanced at each other. Jordan whispered his thoughts to me throughout the film. He was like a less amusing version of... What are they called? The robots from Mystery Science Theatre 3000. A less amusing version, if that's possible."

Jordan Alvarez: "I wasn't trying to be amusing. Just conversational."

Madeline Hart: "Within fifteen minutes of the opening credits, we were shown an exterior shot of the Amy Adams' characters' house. There was a small crane outside. Maybe a tractor. It was sitting next to a sculpture, a Jeff Koons Balloon Dog, as if to imply its recent addition to the property.

Jordan whispered at me, and said..."

Jordan Alvarez: "I found it unrealistic at the time, given my experience of the world, that a woman who lived in that kind of house, a woman with that kind of money, would put an inflatable dog in her back yard.

It looked inflatable to me."

Madeline Hart: "He said, 'If that's supposed to be classy, then my apartment's a goddamn palace of fine art.'

I didn't think much of his comment, other than that it was douchey or whatever, until later in the film, when the Amy Adams character was shown walking through her art gallery, and came across a young bull, suspended in formaldehyde and pierced by arrows – what was obviously Damien Hirst's Saint Sebastian, Exquisite Pain.

Jordan nudged me and rolled his eyes. He said, 'My uncle's got one of those in his garage.'"

Jordan Alvarez: "My uncle is a huntsman from West Virginia. He'd collected dead animals since he was a kid. I'd stayed a week with him when I was fifteen, so that I could learn to shoot a bow and arrow. He'd showed me a fox in a jar that had a twig shoved through its mouth."

Madeline Hart: "By the time we left the theatre, I'd crafted a fantasy that I'd hoped would be fulfilled:

Jordan came from money,
from an art background,
and from a family whose
relatives could afford a
Damien Hirst.

I asked him, after dinner and before my Uber arrived, because I'd had just enough to drink and found the courage... I asked him how much he was worth."

Jordan Alvarez: "If my memory serves me right, Madeline, you told me that you would sleep with me if I answered correctly."

Madeline Hart: "Next slide, please."

An iPhone picture of Madeline Hart, heavily intoxicated, appears on the projection screen.

Jordan Alvarez: "You were hot, but I wasn't planning to see you again, based on your movie recommendation and the ninety dollars worth of wine you'd ordered with dinner, and asked... I mean, demanded that I pay for.

So I thought I'd hit it while I had the chance."

Madeline Hart: "By 'it,' he means me."

Jordan Alvarez: "I thought that having sex with you would be the best possible outcome of the night. So I suggested a number that might have exceeded my net worth."

Madeline Hart: "He told me that he was worth $2 million, and that he planned to earn more. Much more. In the coming years."

Jordan Alvarez: "I'd just launched a vape cartridge delivery app called Vape Cartridge Delivery App.

I thought, with California's recent – at the time – legalization of marijuana, that a 200,000% increase in sales wouldn't be that unrealistic. I mean, it was exciting to imagine: slinging THC-infused cartridges to every vape head with an iPhone."

Madeline Hart: "He was, at the time, a bartender. By profession."

Jordan Alvarez: "You were unemployed. By profession."

Madeline Hart: "I believed Jordan, because... I don't know.

I was drunk, and poor, and had big dreams, and I'd been horny enough to fuck him, no matter what he'd said. Even though he insisted that we go back to my place, because his 'estate was in the midst of renovation.' Even though he'd previously mentioned that he lived in an apartment.

And no, I wasn't on birth control.

And yes, I let him cum inside me.

And I don't remember whether I'd planned that out or not.

Next slide, please."

A picture of a sonogram appears on the projection screen.

Madeline Hart: "Two months later, I was pregnant.

I knew that Jordan was the only man I'd slept with, all year, without protection."

Jordan Alvarez: "I told you to get an abortion. Even if I wasn't the father. Because of global warming, right? Because of Donald Trump, right? Because of our responsibility to the planet, which you didn't seem to care about."

Madeline Hart: "I told him that my family was very conservative, and that they'd expect us to be wed. I presented several options. The sham marriage, I believe, was my favorite.

I gave him the option of buying me a house, on the west side, on the opposite side of town, so that we wouldn't have to see each other, and of allowing me a monthly stipend for the baby."

Jordan Alvarez: "I'd gotten a kind of slutty vibe from you on our first night together, and felt one hundred percent confident in telling you to fuck off. I was sure I wasn't the father."

Madeline Hart: "A prenatal paternity test proved him wrong."

Jordan Alvarez: "I told you that my family was ultra conservative. More than yours. More than any I'd met. I said that they'd cut me off from the will, and from all the money you wanted, if they found out how I'd knocked you up out of wedlock.

Of course, it was all a lie. But I'd meant to force your hand.

I recommended an abortion. A second time. Fully paid for."

Madeline Hart: "I proposed that we be married right away."

Jordan Alvarez: "I stopped answering your calls."

Madeline Hart: "I stalked his Facebook page, and found each of his family members, and cross-referenced their names with physical addresses that I'd dug up online. I sent them each an invitation to our wedding, which had yet to be arranged."

Jordan Alvarez: "I went to the police."

Madeline Hart: "I told the officers who showed up at my front door that the father of my child... That the father of my future child was trying to shirk his responsibilities."

Jordan Alvarez: "Finally, I admitted that I'd lied on our first date; that I wasn't a millionaire, or even close."

Madeline Hart: "I was, by that point, in my third trimester, and beyond the legal requirements for terminating my pregnancy.

I asked for a bank statement to be sure that Jordan wasn't lying. To find out for myself whether or not he was broke.

Then I spent two weeks in bed, crying. Because I'd gone through so much effort, and to have a middle-class child; a liability; a pest."

Jordan Alvarez: "I spent a lot of time vaping and meditating in my favorite gaming chair, and considering how my life would change forever.

'Why not be a father,' I said to myself, 'if I'm going to have a kid?'"

Madeline Hart: "Where I come from, a father – a good one – supports his child. Jordan's ability to offer support was inherently compromised.

The Vape Cartridge Delivery App was only the 1,507[th] business in Los Angeles to attempt to sell marijunana, in vape form, to the local consumer. Competition had killed his business before he'd even opened shop."

Jordan Alvarez: "I was still a bar tender, and made my wage and tips from that.

Plenty of people had raised their children on less."

Madeline Hart: "Next slide, please."

A picture of a Madeline Hart, on a hospital bed, red faced and sweating, appears on the projection screen.

Madeline Hart: "The image you see here was taken by my husband, Jordan Alvarez.

You'll notice the blurriness and poor composition, and how he's chosen the less flattering side of my face."

Jordan Alvarez: "I was under a lot of pressure. You were screaming at me to leave."

Madeline Hart: "I was giving birth."

Jordan Alvarez: "To our child."

Madeline Hart: "In the midst of my suffering... And yes, childbirth is made up entirely of suffering... I made a promise."

Jordan Alvarez: "It hasn't quite turned out true. But yes, as our child, Penelope, stuck her head out from your cunt, you promised to ruin me."

Madeline Hart: "Next slide, please."

A picture of Madeline (in a wedding dress) and Jordan (in a tuxedo), standing together in a courthouse, appears on the projection screen.

Jordan Alvarez: "I received a call one night from your father. God knows how he'd gotten my number."

Madeline Alvarez: "Another example of my husband's stupidity. I obviously told my father how to reach him."

Jordan Alvarez: "Your father talked about the responsibility I'd taken on, and asked if I was willing to 'step up to the plate.'

I said that I'd given it some thought, and that I would do the right thing. After all, my dad had disappeared shortly after I was born. I knew how it had affected me. No matter how I felt about you, I didn't want to be a deadbeat.

Your father asked what I planned to do.

I said that I would ask for your hand in marriage, and that I would do my best to provide for our child.

He seemed pleased to know that we were on the same page."

Madeline Hart: "My father called me the next day, and said that he would no longer be supporting me. Financially."

Jordan Alvarez: "I bought an engagement ring at the mall, and made reservations for two-and-a-half at the Outback Steakhouse.

You agreed to come to dinner with me, and to bring along Penelope. As long as I paid."

Madeline Hart: "What could I say? I was hungry."

Jordan Alvarez: "After appetizers, I got down on one knee and asked for your hand in marriage.

You didn't give the answer I was hoping for. But it was close enough."

Madeline Hart: "I don't know what more he could have expected from me. I said, 'Yes,' but with conditions.

For fuck's sake, I was proposed to by a man with blooming onion dip on his shirt."

Jordan Alvarez: "You asked if you would be able to stay at home, with Penelope, and work on your art career, and whether I would provide for our family. You also asked to keep your last name."

Madeline Hart: "I felt that I was making real progress with an abstract photo series of Penelope's dirty diapers. My friend... Well, my acquaintance, who I think worked as an art dealer, said that they had potential."

Jordan Alvarez: "I told you that I would do the best with what we had. As long as you would too."

Madeline Hart: "Next slide, please."

A picture of Vanessa, with her two-year-old child in lap, holding a small Jeff Koons Balloon Dog, affixed to a porcelain plate.

Madeline Hart: "My friend, Vanessa, who I hadn't spoken to since before my pregnancy, texted me a picture of herself, and her ugly daughter, Ambrosia, and a real-life Jeff Koons sculpture. One of the small ones that comes attached to a plate.

The text read, 'Finally bought one of those balloons dogs. Ernst thinks it's wonderful, and Ambrosia can't stop staring at it! Thanks for the recommendation <3 <3 <3.'

This was right after my marriage to Jordan.

Needless to say, I was furious."

Jordan Alvarez: "I didn't know what you were up to at the time.

On the eve of Penelope's first birthday, you asked if you could borrow my debit card. You said that you wanted to buy Penelope some presents."

Madeline Hart: "I hadn't forgotten my promise, and I hadn't given up on my life just yet.

I waited for Jordan to come home from work, so that he could watch our daughter open gifts."

Jordan Alvarez: "I'd just purchased a Canon XC10 4K prosumer camcorder, so that I could start making social media content for my Vape Cartridge Delivery App, and so that I could capture a few quality moments of our daughter growing up."

Madeline Hart: "I knew that Jordan had taken out a small, $10,000 loan to help reignite his business, and that he'd spent $2,000 on the video camera.

I spent the rest on a Jeff Koons Ballon Dog plate for Penelope.

Well, the dog was more for Jordan. To ruin him, of course.

Next slide, please."

A still frame from the video installation, Baby with Jeff Koons Balloon Dog, appears on the projection screen.

Madeline Hart: "You'll see, on the screen, Penelope with a Jeff Koons Balloon Dog in her mouth, like a pacifier. I'd removed it from the plate and allowed her to play with it. So yes, it was my idea."

Jordan Alvarez: "I thought it was just a regular toy. Until you told me that you'd spent $8,000. As a joke."

Madeline Hart: "It was near perfect timing. Jordan was holding the video camera. His face turned white. Penelope bit into the head of the Balloon Dog, and its body fell and shattered on the floor.

I couldn't stop laughing."

Jordan Alvarez: "You grabbed a bag of luggage and headed towards the door. You said that you'd met a man on the internet, and that you'd planned a weekend get-away together."

Madeline Hart: "Yes, I found a man named Richard on SugarDaddy.com, and he'd offered to take me to a Mexican resort. Tinder had become useless for my affairs. I needed an upper class man if I was going to expand my sense of worth."

Jordan Alvarez: "I didn't even know you were having affairs."

Madeline Hart: "Of course he didn't."

Jordan Alvarez: "That weekend was probably the worst of my entire life."

Madeline Hart: "Not because of me."

Jordan Alvarez: "Not entirely because of you. I hadn't fallen in love, exactly. But I enjoyed your company. At least, when you were naked and asleep."

Madeline Hart: "Can you imagine him a father? A creep who talks like that?"

Jordan Alvarez: "I was wrecked, okay? Distraught. Depressed. Whatever you want to call it.

I ignored Penelope longer than I should have. I didn't notice the piece of Jeff Koons' Ballon Dog lodged inside her throat."

Madeline Hart: "Penelope died on Jordan's watch. That's an important part of the story.

And he was crass enough to turn her into this.

Next slide, please."

A picture of the one-year-old child, Penelope, stuck with arrows, and submerged in a tank of formaldehyde, appears on the projection screen.

Jordan Alvarez: "You have to understand. It was meant to be sentimental. Even sweet.

Come on... I grieved all day, and while you were fucking some fat, old man."

Madeline Hart: "I was probably on an airplane most of that time. Richard took a Xanax and fell asleep. So there was definitely no fucking. Not on the plane."

Jordan Alvarez: "You wouldn't answer your phone. Not for the entire weekend."

Madeline Hart: "Should I have expected him to kill our daughter?"

Jordan Alvarez: "I'd lost the most important person in my life, and didn't want to lose another.

It seemed that you were gone because I'd stopped paying attention. Because I'd never shown an interest in anything you liked."

Madeline Hart: "He pretends that we had a past worth saving."

Jordan Alvarez: "I looked at your desk, and the books you'd stacked on top of it – all of them by artists I'd never heard the names of.

I recognized a piece from one of them. It had been in the film you took me to see on our first date."

Madeline Hart: "Our only date."

Jordan Alvarez: "It was that Damien Hirst with the young bull shot by arrows. Saint Sebastian, Exquisite Pain. I was wrong to make fun of it."

Madeline Hart: "I fucking hate Damien Hirst."

Jordan Alvarez: "You can't judge someone by the way he chooses to grieve. That's what our therapist says."

Madeline Hart: "No one on earth would shoot their dead child full of arrows."

Jordan Alvarez: "No one but me."

Madeline Hart: "Right."

Jordan Alvarez: "Which is why I'm the artist and you're a hack."

Madeline Hart removes her shoe – a Stuart Weitzman stiletto – and swings it, like a hammer, at Jordan Alvarez's head.

California Institute of the Arts campus security rush to separate the spouses.

Judy Fiskin, the American artist and professor of photography and media at the California Institute of the Arts, returns to the stage and to the microphone.

Judy Fiskin: "A round of applause for our guests, Madeline Hart and Jordan Alvarez. Their works, Baby with Jeff Koons Balloon Dog and Saint Sebastian, Our Abandoned Child, are currently on display at The Geffen Contemporary. And Madeline Hart's solo exhibition, A Scatological Examination of Infancy: birth to one-years-old, opens this November at the Fahey/Klein Gallery in Los Angeles."

Madeline Hart fights her way back to the microphone.

Madeline Hart: "I'd like you all to know that Jordan's presence here tonight is a result of contractual obligations, and that we're quite far along in our divorce proceedings, and that..."

The microphone cuts out before Madeline can finish her sentence.

The house lights turn on.

There's a slow clap from the audience, and a standing ovation from at least two in the crowd.

D'SCORPIO'S

as told by Ariel Rosenberg
transcribed by Chad Fjerstad

I lost my virginity to a prostitute in Mexico City when I was 13 years old. Not exactly my proudest moment, but, the details are as follows.

It was at this place in the Condesa district called D'Scorpio's, which fronted as a hair salon. I had been staying in the area at my aunt, uncle, and cousin's house for the previous 8 months, attending the local school for Americans. It was my first time away from my primary family and I had a bunch of milestone experiences while I was there. My first fight, my first makeout, and this.

The previous day was intended to be the big one but it ended up getting postponed. Gaz was a family friend who was supposed to be picking me up at 5 PM. I had been nervously stirring about the house for two full days in worried anticipation of the night ahead.

When Gaz arrived, his friend David hopped out of the backseat and ushered me into the car. There was a driver and the three of us.

I was whisked off to Bosques de las Lomas. As soon as we reached the roundabout, David urged me to pull my pants down and begin masturbating. He was trying to clarify that the moment I came, that'd be the end of it. I refused to wank myself then and there, so I'd have to take my chances. My concerns were less about performing adequately and more about getting past the general hump. I stared out the car window the entire ride, which seemed to be over in an instant.

We double parked and I made my way to the front desk where I was greeted by a mock nurse with a fake mole. Or, maybe she was supposed to be a secretary. She had glasses on and shit, and looked to be in about her late 20's.

"I'm sorry," she said, "You have to be 13 years or older."

I knew I looked young for my age. I was a late bloomer. I was very small, about 4'9", and came off a lot like a real world Leave It To Beaver.

"I am 13," I said.

"If you're 13, I'm 80."

Those words brought instant relief to my nerves. I strolled out of the establishment joyously thinking I wouldn't have to go through with this after all. Outside, I shared the results with the boys. Gaz immediately darted inside to the front desk while David interrogated me. Soon, David dragged me back in.

An argument ensued at the front desk. I took that as a cue to remove my self from the hubbub and head back to the car. I looked up at the night sky, hoping still that I wouldn't have to go through with this. Minutes later, they came out, defeated and cursing under their breath. As they approached the car, a menial male worker from the hair salon ran out and started speaking to Gaz and David, saying something to the effect of,

"Hey, hey, we can do this. It's just that we have a government official that's in session right now, and if he were to come out and see that there was a child there, it might be bad, so please come back in a couple of hours or so, and we can accommodate you."

It was clear to me that Gaz and David had laid down a hefty sum in order for this opportunity to occur. It had been reconsidered. I didn't bother to really process with the rest of what the guy was saying, but it was enough to make me rest my worries. At this point I was resigned to the reality that I would never lose my virginity, ever.

We all got in the car and headed to Vip's for a bite. Dinner was quiet. There was a hushed tone. I happily chewed on my burger and had a very satisfied look on my face, thinking we'd be heading back to the house after we finished eating.

In the car, I noticed we were going back the way that we came, and spoke up immediately,

"Where are we going?"

"To D'Scorpio's you idiot," they said.

"What?"

As soon as we pulled up, the male worker from earlier ran up to the car and ushered me in with no hesitation.

I was whisked up to the front desk where there was a girl waiting for me. She introduced herself as Sara and was probably in her mid 20's. She had a short black skirt. Very svelte. Mild features. Curls in her hair. Almost had a soul glow to it. Her eyes were partially rolled in the back of her head. She seemed like she must have been high on something. She was biting her lip softly. Suddenly, she started putting on an act. Without prompt, she approached me and put her hand on my cock.

"Are you ready for a good time, big boy?"

"Uhhhhh, yes," I said.

I was told to go sit in the closest room, just beyond the front desk, and to wait. The door slammed shut behind me and I found myself alone in a barren, featureless room lit only by a single red bulb. The red glow permeated the dim atmosphere. The floor was carpeted with a rugged matted carpet. In the center of the room was one of those beds you'd see in a doctor's office, with the sheet over it. Next to that was a lazyboy type seat and a small coffee table with a stack of dirty magazines on it. In the opposite corner of the room was a shower stall that was improvised to say the least. To my left and on the floor was an elongated rectangular mirror, leaning up against the wall.

As I sat there in my boxer shorts, with my pants on the floor, my nerves instantly lifted and I was ready for the task. I made myself at home and started flipping through the magazines. Before I knew it, Sara entered the room,

"Why don't you take those boxers off and come sit up here on the bed?"

I pulled down my boxers and hopped up onto the sheet. After briefly carressing my inner thigh, she stretched a condom over my erect penis, then whispered under her breath,

"Now don't you cry on me."

Upon hearing this plea, I went limp. There was hesitation in my mind now. It became clear to me that Sara was a God-fearing slut who thought she was going to Hell for having sex with a child. I couldn't have been more emasculated in that moment, though it wasn't something I was entirely used to to begin with. Puberty came late for me. What little hair I had on my dick curled up like Luigi's mustache, on the corners. I barked back in short order,

"I'm not gonna cry on you! What do you mean? I'm not gonna cry. Don't say that."

I could tell that this was of little comfort to her, but she aquiesced and said,

"Right, right, right. You're a big boy."

She tried to assure me how big my dick was, and that made me feel even worse. I didn't need to hear that either.

At this point, the condom was on, my penis was half erect, and I decided to focus on the task at hand. We moved from place to place, from the bed to the floor. We did it from behind, we did it missionary, we did it from the side. To be frank, I was starting to surprise myself with my performance abilities but I think it had more to do with the fact that the condom stifled most of the sensation. It wasn't too long before she showed blatant signs of exasperation.

She kept on asking me,

"Have you cum yet?"

Eventually she took off the condom and focused on wanking me off. I had many thoughts running through my head. Don't cry on me was echoing through my thoughts, as was my growing awareness that this wasn't the holy pleasant experience it was supposed to be. I tried to stay focused on trying to get off in order to get out of this as quickly as possible, and spare her any more damnation. Her wanking picked up in pace. I had to grab her hand and tell her to slow down. At this point, I pushed her hands off of me and took matters into my own hand, closed my eyes, and desperately tried to cum as quickly as possible. There's an art to wanking, no need to be furious.

She watched in tense anticipation for the spilling of my seed. At the point of climax, I could tell this was going to be a frustrated and forced ejection. When I actually came, very little semen popped out the top.

"That's it?" she said.

"Yeah, that's it," I said.

We both heaved in relief.

We got up and went to the shower, her fears having been extinguished. I was relieved on a whole new level. I did it. I got past the hump. As she scrubbed my balls, I chirped out boastfully,

"See, I didn't cry on you. I told you."

45 minutes had passed since I entered the chamber. Throughout the proceedings, I had intermissably heard bussling at the door. I hadn't realized that my friend's had been standing at the door the entire time, expecting me to come out within minutes of entering. The moment I exited, I was greeted with open arms and jaws ajar.

"What the hell, man? That took 45 minutes," said Gaz.

"We were convinced that twenty minutes in, she would come out with you sleeping in her arms," said David.

I strolled past them dismissively and made my way to the car.

3-6 AM PST

by Rachel Plotkin

You've been playing this game with yourself recently where you come home at 3 AM, often drunk, and ferret around in the dark for a t-shirt to sleep in that's not your ex boyfriend's.

You always lose because most of the shirts are his. It's hard to remember a time when the shirts weren't mostly his, but there had to be one, since you did exist before him.

So you resign and put one on because you hate sleeping naked. Sleeping alone is one thing but you always get too hot or too cold without a t-shirt. After losing the game you can't sleep and you stay up until 6 AM. It's worse to fall asleep before you're really tired because you've been having dreams about him where you get back together each night and break up again every morning. If you stay awake long enough, the dreams don't happen.

At 6 AM, the pair of dogs that live in the RV outside your house start barking to be let out. At 6:05, they both shit in the patch of grass in front of your house. The 45-foot supersized RV has been there for a month and nobody's doing anything about it so you resigned again. Nobody cares about the RV because you live in a sweet pocket of Los Angeles where the parking regulations are few and far between. The Internet is shit, but rent is cheap and you have a pretty good deal.

Between 3:30 and 6, before the RV dogs start barking, you start to think of everything that went wrong this year. It wasn't right with him from the day you both "swiped right" on a dating app, but yin and yang you'd always say! Opposites attract: a constant refrain. "You seemed so happy together," your family said when they heard the news.

You can't help but wonder if everyone is happier than you or just better at lying about it. Surely everyone on Instagram is lying about it. After all, you were.

At 4:47 you consider sending a text, apologizing, swearing you'll be different. You won't prioritize your career, you'll commit, you'll meet halfway, you'll move in this year, you'll make time, you'll go to the Westside for lunch. Everything he wanted. You've deleted his number, but all you have to do is type "R" and the phone fills in the rest. How is anyone really supposed to move on when technology remembers everything? You know you can't send that text because it's late at night and he'll say you're drunk even though your buzz has mostly worn off by now.

You hate lunch on the Westside and you don't want to live together but you fear that sex will never feel as good again, and nobody will be nice to you again, and who would even want to anyway?

It's 5 AM now and you think about your career. You put it first this year and look how it turned out. You're just like your mom. Isn't it funny how we repeat our parents' mistakes before we even fully know what they are?

You got fired in a Friday morning phone call on your way in. Afterwards, you had to ask for shifts back at your old job. You didn't have a problem going back there, the work is easy and pays well. It's just that after 3 and a half years in LA you thought you'd be somewhere else by now.

You could move back to Chicago of course, but all your old friends are still miserable and they do too much cocaine. I mean you like to party, but not like them, you tell yourself. Plus, you'd rather be miserable here and have the freedom to wear an ex's t-shirt year round.

"Good to have you back," your coworkers said at the bar. You laughed and told them you hated your writing job at the agency, but it wasn't really all that funny. Although you did hate the job at the agency - getting bossed around by trust fund kids and tediously writing Tweets for 10 hours a day - the whole thing still wasn't very funny.

6 AM. The dogs start barking right on cue and you consider burning the RV to the ground.

Instead, you gather all the shirts, the ones that aren't yours, and bring them out to the trash.

6:06: The dogs pinch off the loaf as you close the lid.

Fuck the Westside.

SITTING

by Evan Sinclair

She adjusted her posture, and with each squirm he could hear her chair bend, crick, and let out sounds of tension, like bare footsteps over 100-year-old floorboards. It absorbed all his attention, as it always had. For the last 12 years, he'd lose focus watching her body apply pressure to different surfaces. She asked him what the matter was and he didn't catch it at first because all he could think about was if the side of mozzarella sticks they'd ordered would cause their mattress to sink more that night. So instead of asking her to repeat herself, he answered the wrong question and told her he had no clue whether or not they had gotten their parking validated. She asked her first question again, sternly, and he responded that nothing was the matter, though that wasn't the case. He certainly had some anxiety about this dinner he'd put together and was unsure when the right time to ask the question he was dying to ask her would be: if she would sit on him.

It seemed so simple to put into words when he thought about it, over and over, nearly every day since they'd met. It's just undulation and wiggling the mouth, lips and tongue, and squeezing the breath from your lungs to your diaphragm, and the words should pour out like juice from an orange underneath a slow moving tire. But years of self-shame and the possibility of a crushing blow to his ego halted this request. He could see it now; perfect family torn apart after stupid, stupid man asks sweet, robust wife to sit on him so he can jerk off and finally have a gratifying sexual experience. Unsure of exactly when to do it, he knew that it had to happen tonight or else he'd explode like a piñata, but a piñata raining therapy bills and Lexapro instead of candy. In a Deus Ex Machina moment, their mozzarella sticks arrived, buying him time.

In between bites of their main course, she went on about how Sandy down the road was bringing together a group of parents to act as a sort of neighborhood watch. Mitch and Meryl swore they'd seen a group of gardeners come back to the neighborhood in their normal outfits, off duty, which was all the evidence they needed that criminal activity was afoot. Maybe it was something about the inherent racism of the topic and his desire for her to stop talking about it immediately that suddenly gave him strength. So, he said it. Well, he asked it, but his tone was uncharacteristically stern. She stopped for a moment and swallowed her bite of grilled, farm raised tilapia. To sit on him? To sit on him, why? Now, right now? Was this to help with his back? She didn't understand. He lowered his voice, which was very meek to begin with, and tried to explain that it was for a deeper, more carnal gratification. He went on about how it was a form of therapy in ancient roman times and that there were whole clubs dedicated to sitting in most major Asian cities. She held an about face until a small laugh bubbled up. Her guffaw rumbled into a deep belly laugh and she asked him if this was some sort of joke. Nervous, he told her of course it was. To himself, he agreed that of course this was a joke, his deepest, most intimate and passionate desire was a fucking joke along with his entire life.

Later, as she went on about some new outlet mall opening in Wooden Hills, he shoveled a massive bite of his Cajun Shrimp Twice Baked Potato into his mouth and it got caught in his throat. He tried to wash it down with the house merlot, but that didn't clear the clog. He stood up and gestured that he was choking and fell on his back. She panicked and suddenly a man from the nearby table rushed over, shouting his credentials of having completed the local YMCA first responders course, and crowded over him. The hero straddled him and put his hands together into two balled fists on his belly and began pumping to the beat of "Staying Alive." With each push, the clog rose higher to his throat until it expelled from his mouth like a geyser of carbohydrates. By this time, a small circle of voyeurs had gathered to witness a heroic moment and/or their first corpse. They applauded but soon the moment was crushed when everyone noticed the bulge in his pants. Having the pressure of the hero on his body for such a long period of time, along with the short headedness he'd experienced from choking, had given him an unexpected erection. The crowd dissipated awkwardly, chalking the untimely erection up to a biological side effect of a near death experience. At least, that's what they explained to the kids who'd witnessed the spectacle. Huh, she thought, I guess he wasn't joking.

In their bedroom, she did her best to deal. He asked if she had given it any more thought and she apologized that she wasn't exactly in the mood after almost seeing her husband die. He suggested that maybe it was an act of God and she told him not to take the lord's name in vain and he told her that she was deflecting again and she stopped talking. She rolled over onto her side of the bed, their blankets getting sucked toward the weight of her body. After a few beats of silence, she asked what it did for him. She asked why sitting, had he been abused a child, did this have anything to do with his insistence that they purchase a heavier down comforter? In response, his tone became frantic and defensive. It was a side of him she'd never seen, and quite frankly neither had he. Nothing he said really changed anything, though, and soon they were both fast asleep.

At about 4:15am, the feeling of being straddled awakened him. He looked up and saw her, naked and unsure. She asked if this was how he liked it, and he reached down to her full thighs, his fingers lowering into her tissue as he pulled, and soon she was directly on top of his head. A warmth and incubated emotion overcame him as the cartilage in his nose bent flush with his face and his skull buckeled. He could hear the sound of blood rushing in his head, the faint beat of her heart drumming through her femoral artery, the friction of her lightly unshaven legs acting as Velcro to his stubble. With her entire being pressing down on him, he suddenly heard the faint and indiscernible sound of her voice, which he ignored. Soon he could feel her body bouncing with light sobs as a single tear rolled onto his tummy, breaking him from the spell that overtook him. She slid off and rolled back to her side of the bed, apologizing that this was not something she could do for him. This was not something she ever pictured herself doing and she didn't know if it ever could be.

He excused himself from bed and turned the shower on, where he'd eventually finish himself off using her hypoallergenic conditioner.

She had already left for work by the time he woke up. He walked though their house and looked at all things they'd bought together and wondered what any of it meant. It was a melancholy and melodramatic moment for him that he didn't all too much enjoy, so he put a damper on it. It was Tuesday, after all, and he had to get to Sofa Stadium before the lunch rush.

He entered through the back loading dock, as always, and paid off Julio with a $50. Julio showed him some of the newer models of loveseats they'd just received and asked if any of them "did it" for him. He asked if there was anything of Scandinavian design and Julio lit up like a Christmas tree. They turned the corner of the warehouse and came upon a turquoise, crushed velvet couch/sectional. Julio said it's called, "Üle." Like showing off a brand new car on a game show, Julie stripped the cushions off of Üle to show how deep the carriage was. With Julio's clearance, he laid down in it and Julio tossed the cushions on top of him like dirt on a casket. Soon his vision was entirely obscured, save for a few tiny strips of halogen light that spilled in through the cracks. He told Julio he was ready and soon Üle was loaded up on a furniture dolly and wheeled into an industrial elevator, where he'd be lifted to the showroom. The ride was smooth and took long enough for him to think of the name of the divorce lawyer his buddy had used years ago. He remembered being told that his fees were negotiable but that he often smelled of booze and still referred to Asians as "Orientals."

He felt the rolling of the wheels slow down and soon he was lifted and set down by Julio and three other men, who were instructed to be nice and easy with Üle. Julio leaned down once his men had left and whispered to Üle that he'd be back in a few hours. He lay there and wait, patiently. About an hour passed until a young couple sat down, and shortly after that a group of Japanese exchange students and then a heavy set man who smelled like those pretzels you get when you fly. What a couch, he thought. Üle was truly exceptional.

CORNUCOPIA

by Ingrid Mouth

He'd left home under the guise of a late night studying physics, and she was out on a camping retreat with a church that didn't exist. It was technically Wednesday. Her overstuffed backpack was wedged behind the seat of his car. She hadn't been home in a week.

He wore the cotton lace dress she bought at a thrift store for her middle school graduation a few years earlier. They'd spent the day calling him "Susan" and wandering through used bookstores.

He pulled into an empty parking lot after telling her they were on the way to see a band called Oblong Beef. Without explanation, he parked, climbed into the back seat, and waited. After a few awkward moments of expectant staring and scanning the area for an entrance to the storm drain which was the purported show's venue, she realized this was the destination. She reluctantly accepted it.

They kissed and groped each other over their clothes. The back of her head pressed against the glass. Condensation dripped into her hair. His movements became jerkier and less controlled. His hand shot up and grabbed the handle over the back window for leverage. Straining the brittle fabric of the dress with his erection, he lifted his ass and twisted his hips to drag his groin across her thigh for a moment. His mouth hung open and pressed firmly against her face, drooling more than sucking. He'd wedged her into the corner against the door, dry humping in big, twitchy jerks. His tongue darted out aggressively. She coughed and turned away. He always got saliva up her nose when he was excited.

"You have a tissue?"

"Oh, yeah, sure."

He bent over her knee, playfully dragging the silhouette of his hard cock across it, and grabbed the box of tissues he kept in the glove compartment.

"Here ya go."

He tossed them onto her lap.

"Thanks, Austin."

She stared at the box bemusedly, pulled out a tissue, and honked out a load of Austin's spit.

"You jerk off at long red lights or something?" she said, gesturing with the box.

"No? Hey, are you getting a cold again?"

"No. Probably just, uh, allergies."

"Oh. Then we can still..."

He leaned in to kiss her. She turned away and blew her nose again.

"Uh, that's ok," she said.

He shrunk visibly.

"You don't like how I kiss?"

"No! You're fine. I mean. You're great. I just... We've been making out for hours. I'm kind of tired."

"Oh. I know you're not... experienced, but usually people go somewhere from there. I mean, they don't just keep kissing. It leads to other stuff."

The corners of her mouth pulled back towards her neck involuntarily. A grimace.

"I mean. It's ok. I know you've been... your past and stuff. I don't want to push it."

"I'd like to go."

He looked her up and down expressionlessly. She stared at the floor.

"Ok, cool. No problem."

He climbed back into the driver's seat and shifted his sinking wood back inside his ill-fitting silk panties. Looking into the rear view mirror, he combed his hair down with his fingers, unclipped a small, strawberry-accented barrette, and clipped it back over a wisp of unruly hair. He'd start going bald within the next few years.

She sighed and climbed into the front seat, returning the tissues to the glove compartment. Somehow, he got spit up her nose every time, and it always made her gag.

"Is my makeup ok?"

"Yeah, you look pretty," she said, "It's just... This place feels really dark. I can't get into it here."

He once told her he got off on dressing like a woman because he believed it was innately humiliating to be female in modern society. She'd stopped making out with him for a month.

"It's not me?"

"No, it's just, you know when a place gives you a really strong feeling, like it has a personality? It's like you're fucking the ghosts of everything that's happened there. This place just feels wrong."

"Huh. Hey, do you think I'd be more passing if I plucked my eyebrows?"

He pursed his lips and slid his fingers over his brows. She sighed.

"I could do it for you if you want."

She woke up on the floor of a VW bus in a fit of manic laughter. She hadn't been asleep. A stoned, long-haired man in a woven hoodie sat next to her, cackling and pointing. On the shag carpet between them, a magazine was open to the centerfold of a nude, tattooed man with matching forked tongue and genitals.

"I wish he'd tattoo a face on his crotch so they'd match."

She hadn't intended to speak. She faked an itch to hide that she was blushing.

"You think that'd work?"

"Would what work?"

"I mean, if I had a face, like, tattooed on my dick, would chicks want to see it?"

She laughed again.

"I might want to see it, but I couldn't say it'd make me more likely to touch it."

They were on the freeway. The driver held a tall beer can between his knees and was glancing back at them more frequently than seemed safe.

"Hey, where'd you guys pick me up, anyway?"

"Ha HA! You mean you don't know? You from out of town?"

"No, I'm from here. I just don't remember where I was."

"Oh man. I was going to offer you some of this, but sounds like you've got something better."

He lit a joint and took a long drag before passing it to her. She puffed and held the smoke in her mouth long enough they'd assume she inhaled.

"I was hitchhiking?"

"Yeah, man! You never see hitchhikers around here. We were stoked to find you. Fucking bad ass is what that is."

He scooted closer and playfully shoved her shoulder. She made a mental note to move on as soon as they stopped.

"Aw, I'm not a bad ass. I just get bored."

"Bad ass and don't even give a FUCK." the driver raised his beer to her.

"Eh, I'm 14. I'm probably just at the peak of the whole youthful delusion of invincibility thing."

"Shit man, you're 14?" he shouted to the driver, "Hey Mark, this chick is 14!"

The men were silent for a long moment

"I mean, shit. I thought 16, AT LEAST." said Mark.

The girl's brow furrowed.

"There a big difference?"

"Grass on the playing field. Grass on the playing field."

Mark cackled. The girl felt sick.

"Hey, it's ok, man. You're cool. You running away or something? My buddy Jose's been staying in this hostel by the beach. It's not bad. He could hook you up. Tell him Randy sent you. He's always got good shit."

"Thank you. I'll figure it out."

"Shit man, I'm hungry, " said Randy.

"Yeah, we're low on gas, too."

They pulled off the freeway and into a gas station parking lot. Mark and Randy hopped onto the asphalt.

"You want some munchies?"

"I'm good, thank you."

As the doors of the convenience store closed behind Mark and Randy, the girl walked across the street and sat behind a shrub in someone's front yard. When the men came out, they shouted for her briefly before shrugging it off and driving away.

"Have one for me?"

"Sure, and what's your name?"

She slid the cigarette out of the businessman's fingers and purred, "Irrelevant. But thank you for contributing to the delinquency of a minor."

The man's eyes bulged. A woman in a black wool trench coat walked by, tracing them with her eyes. Her cheekbones were high and sharp. She touched the girl's arm.

"Would you like me to get you a sandwich?"

She gestured at the grocery store behind them.

"What?"

The girl backed away, flustered. Suddenly she felt naked and guilty. The glaring fluorescent lights outside the store didn't help. She flashed a huge, fake smile and skipped away, staying close to the side of the tall building. It had taken her half the day to get back downtown. She walked and smoked for a few blocks before deciding she didn't like cigarettes. Ducking into an alley, she rolled up her sleeve and put the cigarette out on her arm. Her head cleared again.

The alley was narrow and criss-crossed with wires and building debris. An ancient door caught her eye. It was propped shut with a block of concrete, but the lock was clearly broken. She dragged the cement back far enough to squeeze through, and bound the door shut behind her with a string of wire. She turned around. It was an abandoned theater. Light filtered through cracks in the walls and ceiling. The last crumbling half of a hanging balcony jutted out over the open floor. It was quiet. It didn't even smell like piss. Entranced, she ran through the aisles. She walked across the stage on her hands. She spent an hour with her sketchbook drawing a broken sink in the bathroom.

In the back of the theater was a massive bird's nest of mangled chairs. She laid out her jacket in the center, sat in front of it, and unzipped her bag. The produce she'd picked up from the grocery store spilled out the top, and she arranged it in a neat row on her jacket's paisley lining.

While holding the fat end of a carrot in her mouth to warm it, she balled up her panties and dropped them. They were already damp. She gripped the middle of the carrot, hiked up her skirt, and slid it inside herself, fast, accidentally bumping her clit with her palm. Seeing stars, she knew immediately she was too excited for the usual length of the ritual. She pulled the carrot back out.

She snapped the vegetable in half, rolled the smaller, more breakable end under the chair pile, and moved onto her folded knees. From this position, she braced the carrot against the concrete floor and slid her asshole down over the fat end. She sat impaled on it, grinding gently, low moans escaping with her breath.

She tucked her arm under her thigh so she could slide the dry, knobby sweet potato in and out of her cunt without brushing against herself, but the friction quickly brought her too close again. She flipped open her knife, sawed an end off the potato, and stood it upright. She rolled the other half of the carrot under the chairs and lowered her ass onto the potato. She let her pussy drip down her ass, gently pushing in and out, until she could sit flat on her heels again, ass stuffed with yam.

The cucumber was bigger around than her wrist. She tilted her pelvis back and wedged the massive vegetable under it. The tip slid across her wet lips, the gentle motion forming bubbles on it's skin. Then slowly, gently, her hand flat under the base of the vegetable, she started to push it inside. It resisted. She pushed until she felt the walls of her cunt stretch to capacity. She kept nudging, cautiously, until finally she was stretched all the way around the tip. She nudged again. It moved a fraction of an inch deeper.

When she'd worked it halfway inside her, she sat up straight, hands free, using the floor to brace the phalluses inside her holes. Her ankles held them steady from the sides. She bounced once, hesitantly. The rough knobs in her ass rubbed against the cucumber in her cunt. She bounced again, slower, and then again, and again.

And then, sweating, grinding, panting, she pulled black plastic binder clips out of her backpack, snaked them under her shirt, and clipped them to her nipples. Her eyes watered. She bounced higher. She slid her feet out from under her ass, forcing the vegetables deeper. She felt her vaginal walls tear slightly. Her ass clapped against the concrete, sending up small clouds of dust. She shuddered. She grabbed the balled up panties and shoved them against her clit. In one thrust, she screamed. Her cunt contracted violently. Her limbs flailed. She fell back onto her ass and elbows and watched helplessly as the the well-lubed cucumber shot out of her cunt, through the broken legs of a chair, past an old kiosk, and THUMPED into the wall under a window.

As she watched, chuckling and catching her breath, her whole body still throbbing, a hairline crack appeared in the windowpane. Her eyebrows raised. A few more subtle pops echoed through the theater, and then a spiderweb of fractures spread across the glass. Then, all at once, it shattered. A wave of glass shards exploded onto the floor of the theater and echoed down the alley outside. The walls around the window shifted and creaked menacingly. The girl's stomach seized.

"Shit."

She leaned forward, wedged the potato out of her ass, and tossed it towards the cucumber. Frantically, she wriggled back into her damp, balled-up panties, dropped her skirt, and swung on her backpack. She ripped a piece of upholstery off one of the seats and wiped her wet hands and ass crack.

A crash near the alley door prompted her to run in the opposite direction. The theater had a front entrance which was fortunately only locked from the outside. She slipped out, leaned against the row of doors, and looked up to find herself facing a police officer.

"Hey there! Where did you come from?"
She had a small coughing fit. The cop stared at her expectantly.
"Oh, hi. I dunno. Uh, door was open."
"No it wasn't."
Another cop sprinted around the corner holding his nightstick in one hand and a fistful of plastic bags in the other.
"Hey Charlie, look at this shit!"
"Walter, this girl was inside."
"No way, it couldn't have been her."
The girl was frozen against the theater doors, knowing she couldn't run.

"I was just inside the door for a second. I was looking for a bathroom."

"No, no you weren't."

Charlie faced the girl and reached around her with both arms, testing the knobs on either side of her body, effectively trapping her there.

"See? Locked."

"I don't know what to tell you, sir. Door opened when I went in."

Walter came closer.

"You see anyone in there?"

"No sir, no."

"You really need to be careful in places like this. It's dangerous."

"Thank you. I will be."

"No, you don't understand. There are crazies out here. Perverts."

"Yes, sir."

"No, really. Look at this."

Walter held up his evidence bags. The bulging plastic dripped with condensation. Inside the bags were the still-warm vegetables the cop had apparently found inside. The girl glowed beet red. She was certain she still smelled like pussy. Walter affected an instructional pose.

"This one," he pointed at the potato, "It's obvious from the smell that the residue is human fecal matter. Sick, right? We don't know exactly what's been going on inside that building, but a girl like you could really get hurt."

"Hey, Walter, you're scaring her."

"Maybe she should be scared!"

"Just run on home now, ok, hon? You don't want to run into the man who did this."

"Yes, sir. Thank you, sir."

LOVE DREAM

by Dan Pederson

It was late in the year but some friends had thought it was a good idea and had dragged me along. The leaves were down on all but the most stubborn of the trees, the ones that would hold onto them, dead and dry, throughout the winter. Nobody was there. The sight-lines were clear around the entire lake, the big houses were gilded in the evening sun. The parks were quiet and the beaches were lonely.

They kept the car running. The seat warmers and defrosters were turned high. All vents open and all fans blasting heat. They marched down to the shore with towels draped around their shoulders.

I counted down from ten. At five they all dropped their overcoats onto the sand. I pulled my scarf tight around me to fight the lingering wind. Four, three, I looked at the bodies of my friends, unapologetic in their near-nakedness, the late autumn sun setting fast behind the trees on the far shore. Two, slowly now, teasing, as they swore at me from their starting lines. The guys acting tough and angry, the girls cute in their groans and their shivering stances. One, and they were gone screaming down the short stretch of sloping beach and into the water. I watched from where the sand met the grass, sat on a towel that was meant for me. I drank whiskey and watched them play beneath a dying cloud-scattered sky.

You had a dog with you. I asked what it was and you said, a dog. You smiled slight and stopped. You were behind me and when you spoke you looked straight over my head at the fools splashing in the slate-gray lake. You told me what breed the dog was but I don't remember anymore. Nodding toward the water, you said you hoped that I knew those people. I turned toward you and said, yes, I do. Some friends. It was there that I got my first good look at you. A long dark coat, buttoned to your chin, the waves of your black hair swaying in the breeze. You held your gaze toward my friends and from below your fair-skinned features cut sharply against the fast-moving sky. Considering the noises that those in the lake were making, you said that I must be the smart friend. You thought I was smart.

Shortly they came trudging out from the water. I rubbed their trembling bodies as they dried themselves in the car. From the back seat I watched you travel down the far curve of the lake. I, in my layered comfort, reminded my friends of the possibility of warmth. I saw as you began to run with that mysterious dog out in front of you. They asked about you but, to them, I dismissed you. Then they'd gone home and nothing more had come from it

That was the last of the warm days, but we didn't know it. We never know that the best days have gone until afterward, until the grass is yellowed and flattened into the dirt, the lakes are frozen and the first snowfall has begun to bury them. You know it's coming, but you will never know which pleasant moment will be the last before the cold sets in.

I was laid up with a hell of a fever for weeks. I sweat through the bed and in the beginning the sleepless mornings had begun to stretch my peripheral vision inward until I saw in my waking life gossamer visions that were indistinguishable from dreams. I left on the sixth day and the doctor I dragged myself to told me to get some rest.

There were vivid dreams. They were lived in by you. I pieced your face together in my mind amid those delusional afternoons. You were in the water with me, the dog was ours. We met at the wide beach in the middle of summer and the leaves were green but somehow we were still alone. On the sand near the reeds I saw you drop a bright draping towel from your bare shoulders and I saw your long legs as they lead down from the calm curves below your waist. They were legs I dreamt, the pale smoothness, the slightly bruised shin, knees protruding and bony in such strange ways. The image of you there in a dark one-piece suit beneath an open sky. A recurring image. Wisps of a burning mind. It felt so distinctly real, your presence and our closeness, that in my coherent moments I questioned my memory. Wondered if maybe those wet eyes and the light pink curve of those upturned lips could have truly been yours. Sick and in solitude, the blurriness was hard to parse.

I'd thought that coming back into good health would make me feel free again. It always had. The first time you wake into normality following a horrific sickness is its own kind of euphoria. But this time was different. The cold had rolled in as I suffered. In the haziness of those days I kept staring out the window just hoping to see a shred of sun scatter itself through a hole in the dark clouds, but that didn't happen. My worry turned inward. Would this ever pass? Would it ever clear up? A day seemed at first like two, then three, and by the end I could have been convinced that I'd been buried for months. Intertwined with my dreams, I came to believe that when I would, someday, emerge back into the world it would be like leaving a doomsday vault. The lead door would grind open and the world I'd once lived in would be gone, changed. No one I met would know me, no one would even recall that I had existed. I had not died, not been forgotten in any sense. I had simply never been and, as such, could not be remembered.

Eventually I woke up healthy, and the world outside was barren.

My hand imprinted clarity upon one of the icy windows. The glass was covered in a tactile, thick frost. The translucent palm-print trickled with loose water, dropping from around my warm skin and re-freezing. When it became too cold and I pulled away, a crystalline pattern quickly sealed the glass again.

It was the middle of December and it never stopped snowing.

It's hard to remember exactly when you had come to me. Day after day the street was plowed and the pushed snow was thrown off the asphalt and piled over the sidewalk and up onto the stairs of my walkup. I watched as my neighbors shoveled it clear. For weeks they worked until there was nowhere else to put the snow and the entrance to the building was overcome. Through the hallways and through the floors I heard them yelling and pleading, and one after another, they fled their homes, trudging through the drowning snow, though where they went I did not know. By the time we found ourselves alone, I'd not left my place in weeks.

I'd often hold my hand on the glass, testing myself to the pain of the searing cold. To free the liquid from the solid. This is something I would get lost in. I didn't notice the unsettling of the floorboards, the groan of the bedroom door. The kiss of the pads of your feet as you crossed the stark living room. You sniffled and pulled me away. Morning had come and this was the rare day where I'd woken before you. There, in the middle of that room where we spent our days, you stood with my white comforter wrapped around your body. You looked like a marshmallow. You yawned and I saw you do it. It made you look ridiculous, but it was about the most endearing thing I could ever imagine.

I saw you often in this way. You said we were the only two occupants of a lonely world, and in that way I found you to mean that nothing was certain, that everything had changed. You walked my apartment in a blissful calm in those days, often undressed with a blanket draped off your shoulders, the outline of your body suggested in the whirling of the cloth as you moved. Once I found you in the kitchen, eating the last of the dying fruit. It was red in your mouth. Liszt's Liebestraum reverberated from the record's groove in the opposite room and, just like in the dream, you spread apart the blanket and let it fall from your shoulders. You sat perched, open, on the edge of the counter and you invited me in.

Outside a blank white canvas covered everything. The sun, through the clouds, fell flat over the world and impressed upon us a deep and featureless place.

I came out from the shower and I was looking for you. The food was low and the curtains in my room hadn't been drawn in so many days that it was hard to remember what the broken daylight looked like upon the bed frame.

You were splayed out on my thick woven quilt, laying flat and naked atop the long window-side radiator like a cat. The eternally wan light pressed through the matted windows, capturing you like a painted portrait. Smooth fading shadows crested along your body. Your arm was cast across your eyes and it was like you were buried in some unknown woe, but you were simply trying to keep warm. To wait for your turn in the shower, you'd said. That you thought it would be nice, for once, to let me clean my body by myself. That you'd fallen asleep thinking that.

I lifted you from the white painted metal ribs of the radiator and carried you off to the endless dim and the ragged sheets of my bedroom. You pretended you were asleep and it was like when I was a child and came home from a not-so-long trip, dozing to a heaviness that carried itself so far as to make me feign sleep. My father would carry me in, through darkness, in safety. I laid the layers upon you in innocence. I combed my hair in the bathroom mirror and I stared at myself long after everything was in place. Dusk passed and I drank the rest of the bottle and fell asleep on the couch, thinking of you, wondering if you'd moved.

You watched the news on the night the power went out. The icy blue light of the screen smeared itself across your face, coursing and retracting like the waves on the lake. Your lips parted, your mouth hung open. They found another one, you said, the idea of frozen people not as distant as it had once been. The commercials were all palm trees.

When it went dark and silent you held me to you. You wouldn't let me go. For the heat, I need you, you said, though it hadn't escaped the apartment walls yet. We lay together, sweating beneath the weight of a dozen draped blankets, ready for the world outside to come in to us. The static-cloaked warnings came through the ancient battery radio I'd found in the closet. Late into the first night the broadcast began to repeat itself. The loop continued through to the morning. You found a weak signal from a classical station, and we listened to that for a few days until it too was pushed out of existence by the warning loop. Stay indoors, do not light fires for heat. Help is coming.

What little food we had in the fridge had begun to freeze. The toilet became a little skating rink. Frozen closed, I had to break the hand-print window to get to the drifts of snow on the ledge outside. You filled wine glasses with the snow, clasping your hands around the bell until the stuff was melted drinkable. It was served with ceremony. You were gleeful. Dinners of frozen yogurt and fresh water. Desserts of some remaining liquor —the only thing liquid that escaped the winter unfrozen. We were surviving together. We were dirty, hungry, trapped, but it is those days that I remember best.

One night you called to me from the window, your voice jittery. I ran to find you completely outside, crouched on the ledge, beckoning to me. You took my hand and I eased through the teeth of glass that still lined parts of the window sill.

I was met by the complete and utter darkness of a world once constantly bathed in light, a silence so deep that the heavy breeze, wet with snow, seemed only a suggestion. No electric light to pollute the sky and not another person in sight. Cars abandoned along the roads. You and me on a ledge.

We sat and you leaned against me. There were so many layers of clothes between us that once I would not have been able to sense a bullet fired against me but there, then, the slight initial brush of your arm against mine reverberated throughout me.

Upwards, you pointed, to above where the blackened tops of the skyline stood. There were brilliant smears of color. Gold, purple, blue. There were stars. A hole in the sky. An outstanding circle existing inexplicably on a canvas of ash. Behind us, the TV clicked, the screen glowed white. It snapped, flickered away and a trail of smoke lit out from within it. Gradually we watched as the buildings around us and down further began to come to life.

The streets were again lit by amber lanterns. The flood of lamps overwhelmed my eyes, the aperture of my pupils having rested wide open for so long. An ache formed that would last for a very long time afterward.

We rested for hours on the ledge, your face bright next to mine. It was not until we saw the first people emerge from the buildings across the street, burrowing out from snowbanks, that we headed back through the teeth of the window to the slowly warming inside.

The sun began to shine. You spent more time at the window, staring out, talking to yourself. You would quiet when I neared. It wasn't long until we dug ourselves out the front door. Half way through the melting drifts we met the neighbors as they dug their way back into their escaped and long dormant apartments. You wouldn't have thought I'd ever seen a human up close, the way I reacted when they shouted to us. You smiled and hugged them, strangers to you, as I shied away.

Water came back. One morning I woke to you at the handprint window, now replaced and clear of frost. You had showered and you looked different. The woman of the fever dreams, a listless and beautiful stranger. I remained wretched, filthy, still matching the place we had created.

When I had stepped out of the shower and dressed, I found you cleaning, stripping the sheets from the bed, gathering our piled up layers of clothes, throwing out the food that had thawed within the fridge. We worked together to restore things to how they were before. When I stuffed those sheets into the drum of the washing machine I was overcome with a sudden drop, a sense of loss. I could never find a sane way to tell you this.

We started to talk about everything outside, about our friends, our families. You were worried about the dog. You planned to visit him and hopefully start to walk him again once everything was clear. I assured you that it would happen.

You packed the small bag that you had first brought with you when you had begun to stay over so long before. After all the danger, your parents were longing to see you, to be completely assured you'd made it through the icy death unscathed. Before you left, I wondered aloud what I should do while you were gone. "You're smart," you said, "I'm not too worried about you."

Everyone tried to pull me out, to save me. An old friend, a girl from the lake, showed up at my door. Her freckled face was radiant with melting snow, and she looked at me with concerned tenderness. The kind of caring depth that makes you feel pathetic. She dragged me out and I sat in the passenger seat as we drove around the lakes and she told me about what everyone had been up to since the cold had come and gone. We moved slowly, and I responded genuinely. I acted kind, interested. I followed her down Hennepin Avenue, walking through the crowds and into store after store, watched her hold boots up to me, hold patterned white sweaters up to herself, ask questions and smile regardless of my answer. She spent time in the dressing room and I watched the women behind the counter as they typed in the email addresses of customers. I identified their outfits, found the tops and the hats they were wearing on the racks around them. When she dropped me off she hugged me and when she said she was glad to have seen me, I believed her. I stomped my boots out at the top of the stairs and unlocked my door. I unsettled the blankets on my couch, found my way beneath them and closed my eyes.

You came back once and it was almost the same. That's what you said, almost the same.

Weeks vanished.

Rain came heavy, and washed out what remained.

THE WEDDING NIGHT

by Caitlin Dee

Tabitha no longer feared the dark. In fact, she often felt now that she was inconsolable in the daylight. The stars sent whispers all around her as she walked night after night through the dark of the desert.

She was bound for Eros, and could in fact see the tallest and most central mountain among the brief but dramatic mountain range commonly known as the Seven Sisters – it had loomed on the horizon all day and within a few hours she would be at the Sisters' feet.

Lost in a quiet reverie, she listened passively to the stars whispering against the crunch of her boots over the sand and stones. She veered from her straight path only sporadically to avoid a boulder, or a sprawling cactus, or one of the larger gray serpents that made their home in the Pink Desert, named for the mauve tint of the white sands under the Red Moon.

As she listened to the whispers, never articulable but constantly sending her into a soothing dream-like state, she slipped into memories of a sunny day, the last she had enjoyed simply for its warmth and light.

It was the day she had first met Templeton on a rocky shore by the nameless sea that had connected their kingdoms and that she had spent her young life wondering at. She was a young princess betrothed to him, a young prince, and though they had never met in the flesh before they were fourteen, they had been promised to one another ten years earlier. They had only finally met each other hours before her kingdom was toppled by his father's, her father executed, her mother abducted, and she and Templeton had used poorly-understood magic to flee. They had escaped successfully—but separately.

On the day they met, she had anticipated their meeting with a tidal wave of emotions she could scarcely comprehend. On the one hand, she was utterly in love with Templeton, and was almost ashamed at her luck of being betrothed to a famously handsome and kind young prince, considering the luck of her sisters and their marriages to much older and often belligerent dictators.

Besides the obvious fortune of her arrangement, she had formed an early bond with Templeton through a communication system that they'd both stumbled upon accidentally, through which they shared their innermost secrets and grown up together as confidantes. It was a more commonly known form of the Rites known before the Scrubbing of magic and starcraft from All Kingdoms, and one that took them years to become skilled at, but which they still scarcely controlled or comprehended at their meeting.

Despite their lack of understanding for how they were able to communicate, they each had taken great pains to steal time together with their scrying bowls out of sight—simple black bowls filled with water through which they could impress their thoughts upon one another by gazing into bowls of water with intention and in certain locations that facilitated them. At times they could even see one another in watery, ghost-like images through rays of sunlight and dust.

Because of their constant and intimate communication, Tabitha had believed that their meeting would be natural and graceful, and had not prepared herself for the overwhelming awkwardness of being within touching distance of someone who knew every intimate detail of her. Clearly Templeton had felt the same, for when they met privately in a pre-arranged meeting before their public introduction on the rocky shore by her palace, they had spent two hours pacing the beach without more than a few minutes of uncomfortable small talk.

She had been devastated with the prospect that maybe upon meeting her in the flesh, he was disappointed and searching for an excuse to rescind their arrangement. For she had long been somewhat apart from her sisters and other royal women in that she preferred to dress in boys' clothes, and was more eager to roam outdoors and get a little roughed up than to spend much time on selecting the finest clothing or making her face and concerning herself with court affairs. While he had always known this about her through their scrying, they had never yet seen each other in person until this day. She had never felt so aware of her own smell, the dirt under her fingernails, her absence of womanly curves.

Finally, on their hundredth trek from one end of the half-mile long stretch of beach to the other, she found herself growing angry with her own uncharacteristic lack of assertiveness, and then with his aloofness. He was speaking blandly of some adventure he'd had on his horse when she stopped deliberately in her tracks. She was even more perturbed when he failed to notice for several moments, and she had determined to forsake her destiny and her foolish notions of true love to set her path alone into the unknown horizon when he suddenly stopped, turned, and looked at her with a face drained of blood and all pretense.

He had opened his mouth, determined, but closed it again and looked hard at the ground when he found himself unable to summon any words.

Suddenly she was no longer herself, but some otherworldly character of compassion with only a tinge of pity, and she stepped up to him and put her hand upon his cheek. All her fear of his rejection suddenly seemed absurd as she sought to soothe his childlike shame, and she moved her hand into his hand and turned them both to face the sea.

"Templeton, we have a lifetime to become acquainted in this realm where these waters tirelessly strip the shores of my homeland at one end and yours on the other. And in this lifetime, there is nothing you could ever prove to me which I haven't already learned of you from water itself."

It could have been a lie, or a deep truth, but in that moment it was both and it broke their walls down to laugh at the solemn awkwardness between them. The rest of the afternoon became a more typical meeting of young lovers, and their shyness gradually melted away under the sun as it glistened over the turquoise and indigo sea as they laughed at and admired one another.

The memory unexpectedly shifted into the moments after Tabitha's escape, when she had found herself suddenly alone inside of a tree much too large to belong to any woods she had ever encountered, appearing out of an enormous glass bowl containing clear water before an utterly startled old hermit.

While he had seen many strange things in his countless years on Veida, Tomas nonetheless had not been prepared for the site of a bloodied fourteen-year-old girl in boys' attire come gasping out of his scrying bowl at a moment in which he had been deeply immersed in memories of his own. It had taken the better part of an hour and an even better part of his carefully-guarded brandy to soothe her, and another hour to grasp where she had come from and how she had gotten there.

When he had coaxed enough information from Tabitha to recognize her position among the Prophecies that were his duty to accumulate throughout Time, he went about preparing her for the next phase of her journey without hesitation or doubt. He had, in fact, been preparing himself for her arrival, though he hadn't understood that fully as he had done so.

Nonetheless, he had an emerald green tunic and canvas slacks as well as a satchel of provisions for a week-long journey on foot through the desert she was to face alone.

She wore the very tunic and slacks and carried the nearly-emptied satchel as she drifted through the memory; the sudden deep spicy smell of his treehouse and the great pleasure he had displayed when he had learned of who she was. His warm but deeply mysterious home and demeanor were a stark but welcome contrast to the bloodied battle occurring around on the stone floors of her castle only moments before.

She was so utterly consumed in the memory of Tomas that she was hardly surprised when, amidst nothing but sand, stones, and serpents, she nearly stumbled upon a single pink rose that seemed to be growing directly out of the sand, surrounded by a ring of semi-polished white stones that seemed to hold their own warmth.

She smiled easily—the pink rose had long been a symbol of her connection with Templeton, appearing throughout her life in moments when he was thinking of her. It was some side effect of the Rites they practiced together.

"A lovely symbol it is, depicting a delicate demeanor with dangerous defenses."

Tabitha didn't even start but turned instinctively around to find Tomas a few feet away, in the flesh. She had no clue how he could appear out of nowhere like that, yet it didn't surprise her.

"Tomas. I have almost reached the feet of the Seven Sisters, and I know I must summit Eros. So with my provisions lacking, I can only hope you're here to give me some bread, or water, or the faintest clue what to do when I reach the top."

She regretted speaking when he spent a good thirty seconds giggling at her, then laughing outright, and caused her cheeks to burn and her resolve to double. He didn't mind her reaction and took his time calming himself before he told her, quite seriously,

"I laugh because you've never been asked to reach the top of Eros. Forgive me, I forget the petals of the rose bruise so keenly."

He reached out and touched the rose between his thumb and the knuckle of his first finger, and it dissolved into tiny violet and gold crystals before her eyes while shrinking out around the sky and into the ground.

"No, you will not summit the mountain, but walk its inner depths. I wish I could say this is a simpler task. And as for provisions, you fast now to prepare yourself for what lies within."

"And what is that?"

"You'll find out soon enough, Princess."

He looked troubled as Tabitha's courage waivered—she realized that she hadn't the faintest clue what would be expected of her, and felt ill-prepared as a somewhat sheltered and spoiled young woman barely coming of age. The fatherly concern on the old hermit's face finally made her indignant, however, and when he saw her mood shift he smiled again.

"You worry that you're ill-suited for such a task, but I promise you'll soon find your natural stubbornness to your great advantage."

She hated when he violated her thoughts so openly, but he was now her closest ally and her only guidance left in the world. She sighed deeply and awaited whatever riddle he had come to deliver.

"Your husband-to-be awaits you in the mountain, but I cannot promise his freedom. I am not the weaver of the web, but the one who tells the spider's tale. You are the spider, Princess Tabitha."

His affectionate gaze had ended and he gazed with concentration at the circle of white stones. Her gaze followed his and became fixated on the ring.

"This is your task. You must claim your rights as Princess and be married by sunrise. You must claim your kingdom, together as one. Templeton's father, and his father and his father's father have been awaiting the opportunity to claim rights to your kingdom in the hostile takeover from which you escaped into my humble woodland abode. Princess, you are the last in your family's line to remember to practice in the Rites, and should you fail, the Rites will lie in wait for—some time—before they reemerge into a new bloodline by what your doctors would call mutation and your priests would call miracle."

Tabitha's throat was suddenly dry, and she wondered whether Tomas would at least grant her a sip of water. She couldn't take her eyes away from the circle of white stones, she could see the pink reflections, a million glass-shard rose petals in the sand.

It stung at her stomach and her heart thinking of the events of that sunny day, seeing her own father's insides spilled upon marble-white stone. To wonder what fate had become by now of the queen, her mother. Everything around the stones was growing much darker, but the warmth from them and the brightness, the simultaneous coolness and sharpness suddenly growing up around her were overwhelming her ability to breathe.

"You wonder how you could go on, and so the time has come to take the next step. I hope you'll find this Rite exhilarating, Princess Tabitha."

She had already felt her head gently hitting the sand for but a moment by the time he had spoken her name, and suddenly she sat up in the same darkness in what she immediately knew to be the foot of Eros. She was, in fact, knelt before a doorway made of wood that had been hinged to a crescent-shaped cavity in the mountain-face.

She spat on the ground and coughed, shook the sense of heaviness from whatever Rite she had undertaken to arrive so suddenly at this portal from her position surely a few-hours journey away by foot, and even some moments as the crow would fly.

She stood with resolve, however, and did in fact feel somewhat exhilarated as she approached the door. The handle was made of silver and beautifully arched, however when she pushed upon the door with her shoulder she quickly discovered that it was locked.

First gently pushing and pulling to make sure she wasn't overthinking things, Tabitha next tried a simple Rite she had learned when scrying with Templeton and imagined the door to swing open toward the inside of the mountain. It wasn't a moment later before the door swung open and she stepped without hesitation into total darkness.

A candle flared before a hunched old woman with white-hair who grunted at her and beckoned the princess to follow her. They traveled down a long earthen hallway by the crone's candlelight before reaching the next door.

Tabitha passed through many rooms, hallways, and chambers in a trance for what she knew was an impossibly infinitesimal amount of time. In that time, she was undressed, laid bare, traveled to unknown realms, bathed in the waters of other planets, consumed plants that showed her memories that stretched beyond her own life, and was always passing some tests and failing others. Finally, she was losing her concentration when she stumbled through a glass portal with another newly-learned Rite into a strange jungle in full daylight.

She knew, however, that jungles weren't surrounded by glass, yet this one was—a clear and giant glass orb surrounded her and the beach lay just beyond it. There were people gathered around, as though watching an attraction, in seating built into the simulated jungle surroundings.

A bloody and pivotal day had turned into a mysterious but penetrating night, and the sudden appearance of such a crowd disoriented the princess. She remembered her determination.

Suddenly she realized that the crowd was separate from her, and that she was indeed in an isolated area on display before them with the crashing ocean waves as her backdrop. It wasn't a tranquil turquoise sea like the one she had always known, but a threatening indigo maelstrom. She pressed herself against the glass, hardly noticing as a lanky, tanned man loped momentarily to the center of the ring in a black and closely-cut suit to announce something about a Tiger Show to the crowd.

The moment the man disappeared, Tabitha understood. She couldn't bring herself to turn around as she heard a heavy cage door lifted and felt the sudden presence of a massive cat. She could sense without turning to look at him that he'd been starved and deprived of contact with other animals for some time.

Tabitha's eyes looked out at the sea through the glass and she could see his reflection over her shoulder. She could smell the heavy rank of the cat, the hunger, the desperation, the hatred. She was completely defenseless.

The tiger stalked her, the only other heartbeat within the

glass container that imprisoned them. She didn't move from her position, and turned back instead to face the waves. The creature seemed pleased at her acquiescence, and a loud purr emerged from its chest.

The crowd stirred.

The cat approached her and Tabitha wondered at the events of the day. The moments stretched eternally as she considered the strange new but ancient love that had brought her here, recalling her sudden helplessness when finally faced with Templeton in the flesh, with the possibility of his rejection. She remembered her sudden calmness when seeing the fear in his eyes, her unexpected compassion for him.

As the tiger arrived to Tabitha's back, it sniffed around her, down the backs of her legs, then suddenly to the top of her head, then her neck—then with a great snort, started to sit back on his hind legs.

Upon remembering her own compassion, Tabitha remembered her mother—her kindness, her unconditional love, her sweet lily smell, her watery blue eyes. She remembered her mother always keeping cats who would bring her rats and birds, then sleep on the princess's stomach and purr incessantly.

She remembered the cats and the sweet and simple feeling of their purring bodies falling asleep on top of hers, their tiny paws kneading her chest to wake her like tiny rose thorns at dawn. The tiger stood on its hind legs and settled its giant paws upon her shoulders. Her knees buckled slightly under the weight, but she pressed herself against the glass to hold them both erect.

She hadn't let fear overcome her yet, and she wasn't about to behave like cornered prey. She could sense the tiger's own rage and saw her orphaned heart reflected in his. They were cornered, the both of them, but whatever strange crowd awaited their mutual demise with shallow excitement.

He stood pressed against her back, breathing into her face as memory overtook them both, and for long moments the tiger stood embracing her and purring, its massive form pressing into hers. He had forgotten his hunger in the sudden satiation of his longing for closeness. His purr reverberated from his belly into hers, and back again.

Tabitha had closed her eyes for several seconds but finally opened them to discover herself back at the foot of Eros once again, only now the outer door was ajar and gently swinging shut. Tomas's face was looming close to hers, surrounded by darkness, and she wondered momentarily as she realized she was being hoisted into Templeton's arms and carried away from the mountain.

She was disoriented, but relieved to find that the dawn had not yet come. She meant to ask many questions, but as the stars sent their soothing whispers all around her and the crunch of Templeton's boots against the pink sand and the beat of his heart filled her senses, she fell into a deep sleep instead.

NEW YEARS EVE

by Stacey Beretta

I think about that night all of the time. I think about her car swinging around each curve of the mountain road, headlights barely cutting through the fog, music playing loud. I think about her a lot, not because I miss her, but because I hate her. After years of being apart, years of no contact, years after her death, I still hate her. Although, I don't think I would hate her as much as I do if I didn't love her as much as I did.

Teenage love is a fire hot enough to burn you for the rest of your life. I know this now. We met in typical 2006 fashion, on MySpace. It was perfect; we didn't know any of the same people. This really appealed to me because I prefer not to know the romantic history of whoever I am dating; I always described it as "putting a face to the extra space in their vagina." I knew she was more sexually experienced than I was and that too appealed to me. I was still a virgin when we met and I was in a rush to change that. She lived deep in the mountains that surrounded my suburban world, getting to her house was a challenge in itself, long stretches of unlit road with paper thin barriers lining the edges, sometimes no barriers at all. I was 16 years old and had just received my driver's license, I give my raging teen boner all of the credit for getting me to her house and back each time safely. Raw determination.

As the months went on I fell deeply in love with this girl. I lost my virginity to her on April 1st 2006. Her mother was in the next room over so we left our clothes on and just took out the necessary "parts." It was the first time I put a condom on and it was weird, like putting my dick into a snake's skin but that didn't keep me from putting on another for the second and third time after the first. I couldn't believe I had just had sex three times in one day after never having done it before. Needless to say, I was in love.

At the time, I truly believed that I would be with this girl for the rest of my life. We were going to prove that you could be with your high school sweetheart forever and all would be right in the world.

It was around this time that she began to show an interest in drugs. She had told me about doing drugs with the friends she had left behind in the town she moved from and how fun and glamorous one feels under the influence. It was definitely intriguing to me as my father was a cop and until I met this girl, I had no interest in trying any drugs at all or even drinking underage for that matter. We didn't start with alcohol though; we started with high doses of DXM (Dextromethorphan), which is the main active ingredient in most cough medicines. Our cough medicine of choice was Triple-C (for those who know, you know). I remember stealing boxes and boxes of that stuff from local supermarkets so we could retreat to her mountain home to melt in her bed and French kiss until one of us passed out. We used to call it "poor man's ecstasy", but in retrospect, we were getting fucked up like Hollywood Boulevard street people, not cute teenage art kids. I can remember rolling around on the floor, drooling, and one time almost dying in a parking lot after passing out cold only to come to while being carried by two good Samaritans. This was not a good look, but drugs became the glue that kept us together in a world that we thought was much scarier and darker than it actually was.

Interwoven in the drugs and sex were incredibly volatile, angst-fuelled fights. She had a rough upbringing complete with a convict father and ex junkie mother. My childhood seemed flawless by comparison. I never understood what it meant to NEED love; I only knew what it meant to want it. It took years of long drives and cigarettes to understand that all of the times she had slept with other boys it wasn't because she was unhappy with me or did not care, it was that she couldn't stand the thought of rejecting someone's affection. There were a lot of emotional issues that I could not comprehend. However, I was a teenage boy, and I had no idea how to handle bringing your girlfriend flowers then seeing a huge hickey on her neck (Jordan, I know you gave it to her you bastard, I forgive you but you are still a dick). I did not have the mental capacity to find out she and another boy had slept together at an all night ecstasy party (how could I have? I was tripping on acid at a Wu-Tang concert when I found out). How do you come to terms with the love of your teenage life becoming addicted to heroin and trading sex for it when you just started your first year of college?

All of this drama was unknown to our parents, who I have very little memory of during this period of my life. It was as if we just occupied the same house and life within the house stood still. My real life was happening everywhere except home.

When college came around, we went to different schools. I remember leaving for school in the morning and driving 2 hours to her new apartment because she said she was trying to get sober and needed me or that she was going to kill herself. Eventually her lifestyle got ahead of her and she had to come clean to her mother and move back to town. This changed everything. Her mother met with my parents and told them everything she was told so now not only did my parents know that I did drugs and had been for a while but they also found out I was having sex with someone who was at the time an intravenous drug user. The next day my dad took me to get my first HIV test, I was so scared.

The anger I felt towards her ran incredibly deep. She had broken my heart so many times and each time I crawled back but now my mother and father looked at me differently. I could tell in their eyes that they thought I was a bad kid and it killed me. The next semester we started going to the same school together, neither of us lasted more than one semester at our respective colleges. I resented her for that. I felt that she was the one who was fucked up on drugs and I was just doing the right thing trying to care for her, and because of that my academic career basically ended. It was only after her death that I realized that I was just as addicted to her as she was to heroin.

Jesus Christ, how I would cry! I would cry so much! I would cry in my car, I would cry in my room, I would cry to my friends. I was crying all of the time, but I relished in it. I felt like my life was like the stupid indie teen dramas I would watch throughout high school. I thought that the amount of pain I was feeling made the love real and worth chasing. Virginity was something that meant more to me than it did to a lot of my friends. I thought it was special and that her and I had shared something really important. I laugh at myself for being so naïve, at my age now people share their bodies with each other like potato chips.

As the months went on I grew to not even be able to talk to her. We drifted apart. I remember the last time we had sex, it was like shaking hands with an enemy, uncomfortable and out of courtesy for one another. Pathetic. One day we both just realized that we fucked each other's lives up and couldn't justify being together any longer. We remained relatively friendly and I would see her at parties and such but one day even that came to an end. She told me she needed to be with me and absolutely needed to see me, I told her that I was done and would not come to see her. The switch inside her was flipped and she went ballistic. It was the first time I said no to her and the first time it became real to both of us that it was truly over. My phone would not stop ringing, either from her calling or from her texting. It was at this time that things really turned dark. She told me in a series of unanswered texts that she was going to kill herself because of me, she explained that she was planning on taking an overdose of tranquilizers that were prescribed to her family's horses. I felt forced to respond and told her that I was going to tell her mother and I did. The calls and texts only got worse, so in an attempt to save my own mental well-being, I had her number blocked. She was no longer able to contact me.

It was two years later almost to the day that I had the block removed, I figured enough time had passed and she had moved on with her life as I had with mine. That same day she contacted me. There was something different about her tone, it didn't seem desperate or angry, but friendly. Against my better judgment, I agreed to see her. We talked for a little bit, the bulk of the conversation was comprised of apologies from both of us and her telling me about some health problems she was having. I drove away feeling better than I had about the whole situation in a long time even though it would be short lived. It was one day later that the calls and texts started, it was more "You wouldn't even fucking care if I died, why are you doing this to me?" This time I ignored her completely and after a week it had stopped.

Flash forward another year and I am living in Hollywood with a girl who I was very much in love with. Our relationship was very positive and healthy and I was happy. One night we threw a party at our home and there she was. I couldn't believe she had the audacity to show up to my house where I lived with my girlfriend. I went right up to her in front of everyone and told her she had to leave and that it was insane for her to think there wouldn't be a problem with her being there. I remember I was shaking and on the verge of a total panic attack. That was the last time I ever saw her.

On January 1st, 2010, the girl I have always referred to as my high school sweetheart was found dead in her car that had swerved off of the mountain road leading to her home. I'm not sure if anyone really knows if she lost control of the car or if she had driven off of the road on purpose. It was a long fall and at one of the few areas where there were no barricades lining the road, a place she had talked about killing herself before. My friends had called me to tell me that day and I felt indifferent. I wasn't sad or happy, I felt strangely at ease. I know that this sounds terrible but for the first time in years I had total peace of mind, I no longer worried about seeing her around and getting that sick to my stomach feeling, no more worrying about when she would try to contact me next, no more *her*. I was immature then and continued to say awful things about her. It made me angry that people had attached obligatory sympathy to her when I still felt so much hate towards her.

Years of reflection have helped me to finally realize the poignancy of this event in my life. I no longer have awful things to say about her although I still harbor the same hatred and resentment. Through her death I have learned so much about myself and about what our time together meant. I now understand that we were just kids moving way too fast and that is really all there was to it. I think about that night all of the time. I think about her all of the time.

HAND PUPPET

by Johnny Love

I don't know what it is about moving out of a city that makes it's women decide they want to hit you up and ask you to "hang out" next time you come back to visit. This happened to me when I moved out of Chicago for the first time. Girls I'd had crushes on were messaging me so I started making a mental list of who I had to hit up. One in particular I had never actually met, but we were friends on social media and she fit my exact "type", which was girls that look like Gelflings (watch *The Dark Crystal* if you don't get the reference).

A few months passed and I ended up getting a show back home. She was the first person I contacted. I was arriving a day before the date and asked her if she wanted to go out drinking so that I wouldn't have to meet her at the party I was playing. We chose to hang out at a bar where all the bartenders knew me, so I'd look extra cool when they greeted me by name and gave us free drinks. The stage was set - this Gelfling was gonna be mine.

Everything was going according to plan. People kept interrupting us to say hi to me (look at Mr. Popular), free drinks were coming in, talking close, touching each other, making out. We even ended up sneaking off to the unisex bathroom (a place

I called "my office", figuring the amount of work I put in there), but she wouldn't let me go further than some heavy tonguing and my hand down her panties. Finally, she said, *"let's just get out of here"*, and we ran outside to take a cab back to my friends house where I was crashing.

We were making out heavily the entire ride back, and as soon as we got there we stumbled onto the couch which was serving as my bed for the next few days. We both stripped naked, still going at it. I had one finger in her pussy and she was going nuts, writhing around like a wild snake. *"More! More!"*, she begged between kisses, so I obliged her. Two fingers in and she was getting that much more into it, *"Harder! More! Faster!"*, so I pushed a third finger up against her G-spot. I was worried she was gonna fly off the couch. *"Fuck yes, another! Give me more!"* Holy shit, I'm thinking, *two fingers isn't unusual, three is rare, but four?! Alright, lets give her what she wants.* I shoved in the last of my fingers, using my thumb to massage her clit, while my hand was contorted into a claw that was basically gripping her pubic bone. She was completely losing it, bordering on Linda Blair style, screaming in pleasure, and yet *still* asking for more.

It was pretty clear what she wanted, and while I'd never fisted anyone (like any respectable degenerate) I had done my homework. I formed my hand into a duck bill and tried to put the whole hand into her vagina. Lube wasn't the problem, this girl was so turned on there was a very large wet spot forming on the couch cushions, and my fingers were looking like prunes. The problem was that my knuckles could not fit past her pubic bone. Try as I must, and try I fucking *did*. She knew what was coming. She contorted backwards, eyes rolled back, mouth frozen open in a constant moan, back totally arched and toes curled. She reminded me of one of those Evangelicals being taken by the "holy spirit" at some Southern revival church.

No matter how hard I tried, I could not make it past my

knuckles. All this girl wanted was for me to turn her into my hand puppet, but after a few minutes of trying I finally gave up, pulled my hand out, and positioned myself to penetrate her. Just as my dick touched her pussy, she looked up at me surprised, and asked, "Wait, *what are you doing?*"

"I'm about to fuck you," I said.

"But wait, we just met."

WILLY WONKA'S BDSM FACTORY

by Damiano Villalobos

Your entire body engulfed, raped by cinnamon candies, stuffed into every orifice and crevice until there is no more room. A peppermint swirl dildo crammed between your buns, force fed a tub of natural Hawaiian lavender sugar, right from the cane fields. A funnel gently inserted into your mouth and avalanches of sweet cane sugar poured into it, left to sundry in an unfamiliar land, humming birds swarm in flocks gingerly suckling the nectar dripping from your supple skin while you sweat out caramelized sugar. Next you are tied up and glazed, mysterious characters are now sprinkling ginger upon your bound nude body, pink sugar next. Rubbing it into your nipples until they chaff, repeatedly whipping your buns with 5ft long licorice rope, lashing you. Lathering you in dark chocolate violently rolling your fastened body in white powder. Strange ominous dark wave industrial music plays in the background, pink strobe lights flashing, you catch a glimpse of the mystery, gingerbread men & neo-oompa loompas, you are in Willy Wonka's BDSM factory, for he is the master and he only arrives to get the real freaky shit started, the twisted, sick, psycho chocolatier. Numerous gummy bear men approach and beat you unconscious, you wake up (still nude) in a cold empty room, candy canes stuffed into your anus and mouth so you are trapped. You begin to hear a faint giggle and the lights begin to dim. Tightly hogtied, you feel massive hands effortlessly lift you and toss you into a blow-up pool filled with chocolate, rich vanilla chocolate this time. The same monstrous force pressing the back of your head into the pool of sweet rich coco, violently groping, plowing you from behind. You attempt to turn your head, you catch a glimpse of green hair and white makeup, right before your face is slammed back into the thick fudge, gasping for air with each thrust, filling your lungs up with flavored goop, drowning whilst plowed, a sweet demise.

Daddy S

by MJ Brotherton

When I was 22, I worked in an underground BDSM dungeon. As a switch (dominant and submissive), my experience and clientele was wide-ranging. From garden-variety fetishists, sissies and slaves, to medical play, bondage, spanking and rape scenes, I fundamentally forwent all inhibitions and limitations. Towering above all others, there was one special, top-tier sadist. He was a brutal, perverted Dom and He was my Daddy. Street level, He was an unassuming wealthy businessman- trade in His money clip and suit for a leather mask, Daddy was a borderline-personality psychopath.

Because of my age and size, I wasn't a far cry from the little slave girls of His fantasies. His visions were complex compositions of Catholicism, sex trafficking, pedophilia, torture and murder. He planned our time together extensively. Over weeks He'd trade emails with the Headmistress, often without my knowledge in order to magnify my fear and naiveté for when He would eventually come to play out His perversions. Daddy came without warning, late at night. He'd stay for hours, making sure He was the last person I saw before I went home.

I'd heard about Him from other ladies I worked with. He was still a bit of an anomaly at this point, however infamous for His erratic behavior and nightmarish predilections. The longer I worked at the dungeon, the more regular my clients were and the more I craved genuine perversion. These vanilla fetishists, these men who came to get bent over and degraded by women because their stable domestic lives and fragile masculinity kept them from understanding themselves- I was *their* deviation, *their* therapy, *their* desire and escape. The more I understood their psyches and motivations, as well as my own roles within them, the more monotonous and exhausting it all became. I had true perverts too but they were too few and far between. I yearned for real debauchery, taboo, and pain increasingly. When I heard about Daddy S and His wickedness my mouth watered. He didn't yet know I existed but I knew it would just take seeing me and my thirst would draw Him.

It was late and I was cleaning up in the dressing room after my last client before I went home for the night. I heard the Headmistress with Him in the interview room down the hall. I put a bow in my hair, took my makeup off and listened, my heart pounding. As soon as Headmistress shut His door I opened mine. I pretended to have left something in the room where He was waiting to be escorted upstairs. I opened the door and found Him standing. Our eyes met and as His melted down to the little gold cross around my neck, He reached out to me- *Daddy.*

I was presented to Him in the Red Room. He was tying a leather mask on when I was led in on a short chain by my Headmistress. On all fours at His feet, my eyes on His expensive leather shoes, He grabbed me by the by the back of the head and shoved my face into His crotch, choking me against the chain. When He loosened His grip, I looked up into His icy eyes-
"DON'T FUCKING LOOK AT ME!"

He spit in my face and flung me to the ground. *Yes Sir.*

His voice alternated between eerie, childish compassion and sinister mania. It was bewitching how well He could permeate reality. Hours turned into days with Daddy. He was a trafficker, child molester, corrupt priest, necrophiliac, abusive father and unpredictable psychopath. He liked to degrade nuns and children, spitting at us, incapacitating us, threatening us, pissing on us, making us touch Him, touch each other, beat each other- after which He'd tell us how sick we were for abiding. Between cackles He'd preach on how we *liked it* because we were filthy whores and worthless children. Daddy liked to threaten us personally, involve our personal lives and relationships beyond the veil of fantasy. To Him, every divulgence was a souvenir of psychic murder, consummating His dominance. He once ate spaghetti and meatballs off of a nun's bare ass while she was bound to a table. After finding out that she was indeed a mother in her real life, He made her tell Him how she would murder her children, molest their corpses and chop them up into little pieces while He finished off His entrée and spit it on the floor, leaving her naked, bound and crying.

Daddy chained me up against the roaring fireplace on my hands and knees like a bad dog. He walked back and forth,

"Therefore I thee exhort, in view of God's mercy, to offer your bodies as a sacrifice, holy and pleasing to God- this is your true and proper worship, your purpose."

He was torturing my little sister in her cage with a baton, now and again coming back to me and pushing my back down violently when it wasn't arched enough. He held me there in front of the fire until I cried. He took my face in His hand and mounted me, whispering in my ear,

"Pray"

When Daddy hurt me, He *hurt me bad* but when the pain subsided I desperately *wanted* it back.

When Daddy found out I was moving away He was upset. I was worried I would never see Him again. I sent Him handwritten notes and drawings, begging Him to come home. Trying my best to reach His taste for pedophilia, I based the notes off of the drawings I used to make my father when I was a little girl, imagining Daddy getting hard to my backwards S's:

After weeks of elusion, He responded with a promising e-mail,

Subject: DEAD GIRL IN A BOX.

He came around midnight, heavy with wine. In my nightgown, freshly shaven of all my body hair, I prepared to die. They built me a coffin from old closet doors in the basement. Candles lined the dark little girls' bedroom that was my grave and a cathedral choir echoed through the dungeon. Wrapped in a translucent body bag, I lay in wait for my Daddy. Arms crossed, a rosary around my wrist, they finished me off with a dozen roses atop my plastic shroud-

Yea, though I walk through the valley of the shadow of death, I will fear no evil, for Thou art with me. Thy rod and thy staff, they comfort me, Daddy.

His hot breath fogged over the plastic. Mine was shallow, my eyes closed. Another lady watched beside my coffin. Daddy took off my bag and got in the coffin with me. He brought my face up to His, holding the nape of my limp neck. He forced his tongue into my dead, empty mouth. He touched me all over and ran the rosary down my body until He reached the end of my nightgown. His cock grew at the sight of my nubile exposure. My eyes were closed but I heard Him unzip His pants while He kept one hand on my neck. He moaned and lay on me, tongue in mouth. Daddy said over and over again, as He molested my corpse, how pretty I looked, how my body was still warm and how much He would miss me. As my Father Proper, He recited my Last Rites,

"God our Father, Your power bringeth our birth, Your providence guideth life, and by Your command we returneth to dust. In company with Christ, Who died and now lives, may she rejoice in Your kingdom, where all tears are wiped away. Unite us together again in one family, may we sing Your praise eternally."

I don't know how long He went on this way, alternating between words of faith and moans of deviance. Aroused and manic, His hands pressed tightly on either side of my head-

"Wake! Wake up my child! By God's power, open your eyes! I need to look into your eyes one last time!" The lady crouching next to my box whimpered.

"Shut up bitch, I am a man of *God* and this is my child!"

Again, He called for me and I realized that He actually wanted to resurrect me as part of His bizarre ritual. I inhaled deeply and came to, whispering in my softest little girl voice,

"I can't see! Where am I? Why can't I see? I can't move! *Daddy*, is that you? I can't move!" doing my best to cry.

"There she is, that's my little girl, that's my Genevieve!" He said, "See, bitch, she's awake!" He laughed at her and turned back to me; grabbing my face in vicious compassion-"You died *Baby*" He kissed my face softly and breathed into my ear, *"Daddy's here, Daddy's here."* I started crying.

"What did you see, Baby? Where were you?"

"I...I...don't know...I...I'm scared..."

"*Shh*, Daddy's here. Why are you scared little Genevieve?" He kissed me again.

"Because...I'm a sinner and...*God hates me.*"

He lifted Himself from me and, still straddling me commanded, *"SLEEP NOW."*

I was dead again. He turned me over, my weighted arms folding unnaturally beneath me, and He rubbed against me in my box, exposing my virginal ass. He turned to the lady beside me,

"You're a mother aren't you bitch?"

(She whimpered)

"You are, aren't you? *ANSWER ME WHORE.*"

"Y-yes, I am", she said quietly.

(He laughed)

"*Touch her*. Go on touch her! You want to, don't you?"

"I...I don't know..."

"*TOUCH HER* " He pressed her hand on my ass. "*That's right.*" I could hear His smile deepen.

"How many, how many babies have you had?"

"Um, j-just one- my son" Her voice was quivering on the brink of tears, realizing the mistake she'd just made.

He scoffed and lay over me, violently pulling my head back by my hair,

"You hear that, *Baby*? She has a SON!" He cackled in a frenzy, letting my head drop back onto the coffin floor. "You like this, don't you whore? *Feels good don't it?*" They both continued to grope me.

"Yes, Sir." She started crying.

"I bet you'd like to do this to your son, wouldn't you? I bet you go home and do it to him every night, don't you, *mama?*"

He was winning the game- she was helpless. I could feel His hard cock through His voice. He pushed her hand between my legs and she started sobbing. Daddy was laughing and slapped her across the face. He pushed her hands away,

"SHE'S MINE SLUT"

She was bawling and breathing heavily. She was new and inexperienced, pressured by her financial need and desire to please management. I tried to briefly forewarn her before the session. I reminded her to use code words and not to tell Him any information about herself, to remain a safe distance. She was nervous, maybe even scared. I reassured her that she could look at me during the scene and I would code for her if she were too overwhelmed. Truthfully, I knew that Daddy liked the words yellow and orange. It turned Him on to know He was bringing you to the edge. She was going to be pushed and I wasn't about to let her ruin the scene. She shouldn't have been there. She kept looking down at me. I don't know if I would've coded for her but I was worried.

"DON'T LOOK AT HER!" He jolted towards her, raising His hand. She winced.

"Yellow!" She screamed.

He laughed maliciously, "Are you scared? Is that why you were looking at her? She can't help you, *she's dead!* You stupid whore! What do you think I'm going to do to you? What do you think I *could* do to you?"

"I-I don't know!"

"Go on, say it. Tell me to stop, say red, go ahead! What did you think, I came here for *you?*" He laughed, "You think I was going to *fuck* you? *You?*"

She continued to cry as He forced her hands back on me, goading her, whispering to her in His baby voice about how ugly and poor she was, how old and stupid, what a sick person, what a bad mother, 'what a waste of skin' she was. All the while she was whimpering and trying to take her hands off me but He was restraining her. She'd endured enough,

"Daddy?" I said in a quiet whimper.

He instantaneously let go of her. She made a gasping breath of relief that almost brought me to tears. He violently turned me right side up and stuck His tongue down my throat. Daddy was hard, Daddy was angry, and Daddy loved me. He grabbed the plastic body bag and put it back over me. He pulled in taught around my face. I couldn't breathe, I didn't move. I felt Him touching Himself against my body. Breathless and choking, I let Him hold me down, suffocating me. I could hear the lady crying next to me and then there were spots behind my eyes and all I could hear was a ringing sound, but I let Him smother me. I was barely conscious, I couldn't feel my body anymore. I opened my eyes and gasped for breath, sucking the plastic into my mouth which instantly caused Him to come on my body bag. He took His hand off of me and lifted the plastic from my face, collapsing on me. I lifted my head and whispered one last word,

"Pray"

As I lay my soul to sleep, I pray the Lord my soul to keep. And if I die before I wake, I pray the Lord my soul to take-
I am a dead whore in a box- a pervert, a pyre, I'm Your empty baby girl, set my box on fire.

NEWLYWEDS

by Oriana Small

"Adam? Are you okay? We're so worried. I haven't heard from you in almost four days. Are you taking care of yourself?" That's all his newlywed bride could get out before shielding her mouth from letting out her shaking sobs.

"Yeah, beautiful. I'm just staying away to try and chill out. I wish I could come home. I'm sorry. I love you so much." Frustrated, he kicked the hotel chair.

"I'm so sorry too," she wept in agony. "We miss you."

It was too much to consciously bear. His one true love was waiting up for him and he just couldn't stop letting her down. He wanted to be the super human that won everyone over and never lost a battle, or an emotion or regret and Leslie would always be smiling for him. He ruined the best thing that ever happened to him because he had to lie about being on meth behind her back the entire time they were married. It broke her heart to ask him to move out for the sake of her daughter and their health and the family. She must have known about the other stuff too, like steroids, but meth was the deal breaker.

Kelli showed up right on time at the door to his room at the Hyatt. Adam could not be alone under any circumstances. Needy didn't even begin to describe his level of attention seeking behavior. Every good call girl brings reinforcements. Monica, the rockabilly stripper was Kelli's sidekick for the night. They both had fake tits, tattoos, recreational drugs and accepted cash.

While the ladies got situated, Adam slipped out on the balcony to make a call back to his wife. He hid himself from view of the whores, trying not to seem broken.

"Adam? You know what, just please come home. We can work this out. Don't hurt yourself! I love you and I'm desperate," she wept. "Be with me!"

"Beautiful, I love you more than—I swear," he bleated.

"Come home and quit that shit! Let me come get you now, please, baby, please!" Wailed his new bride.

"I will be home tomorrow. I swear that I can." The phone hung up. He sat alone staring into the desert sky. He tried calling back, but it went straight to voicemail each time.

Kelli, the bleach blonde with grown out brown roots, popped a cheap bottle of sparkling wine all over her naked body and shared it with her girlfriend. They pressed their skinny, bruised limbs against the sliding glass door to cheer Adam up while hollering, "Look, babe!" The sluts distracted him from his recent heartache and reminded him that he needed more drugs.

"This is all? Nah, get more. I don't care. Get everything. And let's Jacuzzi," faintly sounding like a party boy as he tossed the whores his wallet.

Monica drew the most luxurious jet bath and gave an honest attempt at seduction while Kelli had balls of dope delivered to satisfy her client's appetite. They feasted on an array of shit and ended up naked in the bubble filled bathtub. This was how hooking was supposed to be, in the girls' minds. No sex, just fill the guy up with drugs while he was going through some emotional crisis and then, you're out of there.

Somewhere between midnight and sunrise, they seemed satisfied in a daze. Still in the warm bath and drinking worse than Korbel from the bottle, they smoked Clove cigarettes and blew it into the bathroom fan.

"I need you guys to shoot me up," Adam blurted, with his eyes shut.

"Who? Both of us?" Kelli spoke for the two.

"Yep. Both arms, same time. All that shit, now," he

proceeded to get up and grab his wife beater, rip it in half and tie both arms off. "Ready."

Blondie wasn't hesitant. She got the works ready and prepared the needles like it was coffee. Tap, tap. Silently, the girls locked eyes and agreed on injecting simultaneously. Spike in stereo. But they need to split to save themselves. None of this was intentional. Not even the fact that they all knew it was dangerous. Nobody should go to jail though. This would haunt them for the rest of their lives and fuck them up for generations to come, no matter what.

What they saw were Adam's eyes leave his face and his body sink under the bathwater. They knew what was happening under the bubbles. The party he'd asked for was over for good. It was all so stupid now and obviously fatal. Fucking morons! Run, scum!

She became a widow that night at the Hyatt. Leslie lost the life of her love. She could not save him ultimately, like she wanted to. Fate brought them together. This was his fatal ending. When police solemnly contacted Adam's bride about his accidental death, they didn't mention any hookers. His car had to be reported stolen, along with all his credit cards and identification. Other than the theft, he had been found unconscious in the tub. It wasn't a murder or suicide, but the accident of a person who was very loved.

HARMONY IN ROTTING

by Chad Fjerstad

When the man met the woman, he had the heart of a boy. But soon, his love for her would ripen it. She beamed with an allure unlike any he had known. He saw her on a pedestal, hoisted far above his meager traipsing grounds.

Though the woman was oblivious of the man's perspective, it took little time for her to sculpt a shared stature in his mind. Her longing for intimacy opened the carnal floodgates between them, at first through verbal hints, then concreted through action.

At lightning's pace, their bond grew into a perilous beast. The magnetism became addictive, hypnotic as a spell. No other form of distraction from the mundanity of their existence could provide the contentment that being entwined could.

After three days of withholding, they gave into their fervor. The man's perception of physical sexuality was immediately expanded upon, admiring the woman's nude figure. Her divinity set a new standard, surpassing the former which was primarily shaped by a life span of consumed media. A pleasant inauguration led way to a torrent of orgastic conduct. The resulting carnality was beyond all intimacy the man had imagined possible.

Whether chemical, alchemical, or otherwise, there was a

synergy manifesting. The sensation that their souls were merging grew stronger with each intimate act. Their tongues pulsed and coiled, as their saliva pushed its way into the back of each others throats. She mounted him, grinding her loins into his. Secretion gushed from her candidly, more with each gesture, cascading over parts of his body and encapsulating him like a symbiote. In her eyes, he saw all there was to see.

When three months passed, they'd hardly moved from the maiden's chamber. The woman lay there with her head in the curvature of the man's arms, peering up into him with her supernatural eyes.

"I want to hear you say it," she said, "I can see it in your eyes."

"Really?" he asked her, "You're sure?"

"Yes," she said.

"I love you," he told her.

"I love *you*," she said.

For three years, the woman made the man feel like a god. His senses told him he induced the same sort of rapture in her.

On the fourth year, the man caught the woman red-handed amidst a pursuit of lechery. She denied all evidence which eventually proved to be truth, making clear that she had been keeping secrets for some time. His heart felt mashed into a useless paste and his soul so heavy with the weight of darkness it felt as if it were seeping out of his body. Day and night she consumed his thoughts, severing his ability to sleep as he retched in nauseous misery. What hurt the man most was his belief that the shared affinity between them had not depleted. When several months of the woman's lascivious romp had passed, she returned to the man with space for him in her heart, just as he felt she would.

On the fifth year, it happened again, but with a new suitor. The man's heart was broken, but only half as vehemently as the first time. Still, he knew that nothing between them had diminished.

On a rather desolate night, the man made way to the bar closest to his home. Part way through his old-fashioned, there was a lull in business so he plummeted into conversation with the bartender,

"The heart wants what it wants," said the bartender, "People'll tell you what you should do based off of these surface rules. From the brain. What everyone seems to neglect is the rules of the brain are irrelevant unless the heart is tended to first. The brain don't work if the heart ain't first."

The bartender turned around and grabbed a bottle of tequila reposado.

"You wanna take a shot with me?" he asked.

"Yes," the man answered, "I certainly do."

Once they'd downed their shots and licked their salted hands, the bartender carried on,

"Majority of people will tell you *don't fuck with fire*. Why? Because, it'll kill you. If you're not careful, right? So, people just walk away. They'll tell you to walk away or *you're an idiot*, right? Well, that's based off of fear. I say *fuck fear*. I say never let fear stand in your way. If there's fire in your heart, you should put on the gear and jump in. Like a mortician. Cutting into death with their scissors. Don't listen to people. Listen to your damn guts."

After several months of pruriency, the woman returned to the man again.

By the sixth year, when the woman involved yet another suitor in her chaotic lewdness, the man accepted the behavior as a cyclic characteristic of the woman. What had become an annual ritual continued to hurt the man, but only half as much each year.

Nearly a decade of romantic entanglement had passed when the woman's most alluring mentalities began reversing. Her self-certainty had morphed into a crippling insecurity, so engrossing that it became the only subject she could speak of, approximately eighty percent of the time.

"I've gained weight," she said, "I'm fat."

"You're not fat," he told her, "You're the most beautiful woman in the world."

"I'm disgusting," she said.

The woman's contempt towards her self would act as a poison, slowly eating away at the otherwise boundless intimacy they had maintained for so long. The improbable sex they indulged in became exponentially sparse.

"You never make me feel sexy anymore," she said, "You never make an effort."

The man would take her to dinner, tell her how gorgeous she looked, and then when he would attempt to initiate sex, she would reject him.

On the tenth year, the woman realized her annual stints no longer effected the man emotionally. He carried on through her movements of outsourced lasciviousness as a concreted independent soul, waiting patiently until she returned to him again, as she always did.

At night, the man would wake up to the sensation of his head being shoved violently from one side to the other.

"You're snoring," the woman said, "And your breath stinks."

Common efforts such as chewing gum and excessive toothbrushing were not enough to put the woman at ease. The man began taking specialized breath pills from the health food store, which were designed to attack the problem at its gastrointestinal source, but even those failed to solve the problem.

They sat in the woman's living room, watching a film on the television. Several feet from one another, the man sat still with his lips closed.

"I can hear your mouth sounds," she said, "And your breath smells terrible."

The man grew used to holding his head at a considerate distance whenever they would converse in close proximity. He also grew used to falling asleep with his head turned away from the woman each night, no longer spooning her to sleep the way they used to enjoy.

From that point on, the woman developed a distaste for a different characteristic of the man each year. The next characteristic she scorned was his wardrobe.

"When I met you, you dressed better," she said, "You have no style anymore. You look like a laborer."

The man made an effort to only wear clothes the woman found acceptable from then on.

"I'm getting old," the woman said, "My youth is leaving me.

117

I'm past my prime. I'm ugly."

"You're still the most beautiful person I have ever seen," the man said.

"No I'm not," she said, "There are a million girls who are younger, skinnier, and hotter than me. It's only going to get worse."

Another year passed. Another unpleasantry came to light.

"You stink," the woman said.

"My breath?" the man asked.

"No," she said, "Your body odor."

The man sniffed his own armpits, and smelled only freshness.

"I just showered a couple of hours ago," he said.

The woman shrugged,

"That shirt is ugly too."

When the time came, the woman vanished with her next suitor.

On one stag night, the man made his way back to the bar. The bartender greeted him immediately upon his approach,

"How's that fire burning, buddy?"

"It's still burning," the man said, "But who knows how long."

The bartender finished making an old-fashioned and gently pushed it out across the bar top in front of the man. Just as the man wrapped his hand around the low ball glass, an inviting voice chimed in beside him,

"Hey. That's mine."

The man turned to see the voice matched by a breath-taking face. A tiny girl stood next to him with eyes that shimmered like emeralds, and skin as buttery as ice cream. Her half smirk ached to go full bore behind an adorable pair of pursed lips. She glowed with youth. She appeared about nineteen, but had to be at least twenty-one in order to drink at the bar.

"I'm sorry," the man said, "I shouldn't have assumed. The bartender knows it's what I drink."

She let her smile loose.

"You can have it," she said.

"I couldn't," he said.

"Please," she said, "I want you to have it."

"Really?" he asked, "You're sure?"

"Yes," she said, "I promise."

The girl was born into fortune. Her father was the owner of one of the more successful airline companies in the country. Once her father passed, she would be the heiress. She was some type of a modern princess.

At bar close, she asked him for a ride home. When they pulled up to her colossal estate, she asked him to come inside.

Through the double-doored entry way, they faced a lavishly carpeted staircase leading to the upper floor. The girl took the man's hand and led him to the stairs, then had him sit down on the third step.

She swiftly took the man's head and pulled it into her chest. The soft flesh of her breasts pressed into his face like a pillow. She smelled sweetly familiar to him. In her warmth he found comfort and grew aroused. The moment he was hard, she pulled back enough to peer into his eyes. Her eyes were apt enough on their own, capable of communicating without words.

She reached down and squeezed him through his pants, flashing a smile after copping the feel.

"Wait," the man said, "Is anybody else home?"

"Nobody else lives here," she said, "This is my house. *All mine.*"

"That's incredible."

She giggled eagerly while unzipping his pants, and began working him with her mouth.

The moment the girl's mouth encompassed him, he was dumbfounded. A blissful sensation surged through his entire body as he writhed in place on the staircase. Saliva poured past her glistening lips and down his shaft as she bobbed up and down with such joyous devotion. He had forgotten how incredible it felt to be intimate with someone so full of enthusiasm, so full of youth.

As each part of her architecture was unsheathed, the man grew more fascinated. He had not been so astonished by a nude figure since he was first intimate with the woman. Even the finest of sculptors would fail to recreate the girl's physical supremacy if they tried.

When finally she guided him inside of her, they indulged in

an outstanding act of inaugural copulation. After she came twice, once while riding him and again while being taken vigorously from behind, she got down on her knees to encapsulate him with her mouth. The girl was committed to providing the highest tier of physical gratification, even during and after the man's orgasm.

Once she finished milking the man dry, he stared down at her in awe. She looked up at him with the most vivid smile, soft coos of satisfaction escaping her mouth. Her presence was so angelic, and her eyes so full of promise. She was truly a divine creature, a young demigoddess in his eyes.

When the act was over, they lie next to each other at the bottom of the stairs, breathing heavily and covered in beads of sweat.

"I love you," she said.

"Don't say that," the man said.

"Don't be scared," she said, "Love can mean so many things. No expectations, but there's a fire between us."

So began a binge of affection, hedonism, and combustible escapades between the man and the young demigoddess. For months, they carried on mounting each other and restlessly drinking each other's cum. The sex was so fulfilling, so incessant, there was little reason to do much else.

New flesh aside, the man sensed the woman would be returning to him soon. The woman always resurfaced with a surge of reignited desire for the man, immediately following her stints, though it became more brief each year.

The man and the woman had sex for the first time in three quarters of a year, which was as wonderful as it had always been. He reveled in the sensory delights that only their bodies in unison could provide. He missed the savory taste of her fluids, the ardent way she kissed him, the way her body retracted around his when she came. Though she lacked the provocative spirit she carried for so long, it couldn't diminish what their sex would always be worth to the man. When they finished, the man wiped his semen from the woman's rump and lie next to her.

"I'm disgusting," she said.

"You are *not*," he said, "You're the most beautiful. You always have been and you always will be."

"I'll just never be as hot as I used to be," she said, "I'm too old. I'm through. I should just kill myself."

"Please," he said, "Don't do that. Don't even say that."

"I mean it," she said, "I want to die."

"*Stop,*" he said, and carressed her hand.

Later that night, the woman expressed a desire to have sex again. This time, the man was distracted by the sadness in her eyes. Overcome by self-loathing, she lie there eyeing parts of her own body, which proved to be an infectious form of antagonism. The man found himself following her eyes, noticing parts of her body which were no longer the sculpturesque formations they once were, beginning to see them in the same light that she apparently did. He couldn't help but compare her to the young demigoddess who he'd spent most of his recent time prodding. The woman was in fact losing form which was visible through the flab in her stomach, thighs, and ass. New bits of cellulite, stretch marks, and wrinkles convulsed like larvae, protruding from her flesh in a way he had never before recognized.

The man pulled out of the woman in an attempt to deter them both from the unwelcome distractions. He brought himself up to her face and pushed himself gently into her mouth. As she began fellating him, he made an effort to be patient, but soon accepted that all he could feel was the scraping of her teeth. He began to lose his erection.

In another attempt to restore their spirits, the man requested the woman turn around. After rimming her briefly, he went to enter her again but found it challenging as her nether region was parched. She reached over to grab a bottle of lube from her bedside dresser, but realized it was empty. They both applied what little saliva they could produce to their genitals. He shoved his half-hard penis into her and began pounding her as fiercely as he could. Mascara-infused tears streamed down the woman's face as she listened to the sound of her sloppy cheeks flopping.

"The fireman!" said the bartender, enthusiastically.

"Hello, good sir."

"How's that fire burning now?"

"I'm not so sure anymore."

"How can you be unsure?" the bartender said, "Is the fire out or not?"

"Well, there are other fires now."

"More fires?" the bartender said, "You can only fight one fire at a time! You just gonna let the old one burn on it's own? *Could kill somebody...*"

After three years of a casual yet impeccable relationship, the young demigoddess asked the man to commit to her.

"I love you," she said, "My parents love you. We all love your art and everything you stand for. We want to support you. You can move in with me. We can cook dinner together and sleep next to each other every night. It will be perfect."

The man simply smiled in response.

"And the sex," the young demigoddess said, "The sex is so incredible, and it will always be."

She leaned in to kiss him with her silky lips, and with that they re-entered an erogenous realm.

With his hand in hers, she guided him to the poolside terrace behind the house.

On a loveseat near the hot tub, she got down on all fours and crawled around with her tongue out, panting like a puppy. The man observed the way her unblemished flesh stayed snapped so tightly to her bones, and grew wildly aroused at the sight of it. The neon lights in and around the water changed colors fluidly, dancing across her figure, adding a layer of surrealism to her lure.

Following her sultry gestures, she went down on the man until he was hard as can be, then mounted his skyward erection. She knew precisely how to grind into him to accelerate her own climax.

The young demigoddess's orgasms were irregular in length. She wailed in pleasure as fluids blasted out of her continuously, for so long that the man often felt disconcerted though still fiercely aroused.

When finally her extensive orgasm was complete, she got down to suck the life out of the man as he came. When he was finished, she curled up into a ball on the loveseat and jutted her bulbous ass up into the air.

"Fuck me again," she demanded, "I need you to cum again!"

The sexual energy was meteoric, so much that it surpassed any need for a typical refractory period. When he came for a second time, she straddled him and whispered in his ear,

"We are perfect. We're going to be so perfect."

The man kissed her and looked up to the stars.

The man lie next to the woman. She appeared so serene in her sleep, as gorgeous as the day he first met her. He gently traced his fingers across her body, starting with her hands then moving up her arms to her sides. He spent a few delicate minutes scratching her back, then massaging her neck and shoulders. Leaning over her, he stared down at her face which he would always see as the most beautiful sight in the world, and gave the woman an earnest kiss on her forehead. Turning to lie on his back, he watched as the gravedigger closed the casket lid above them. Their bodies rattled next to one another as they were slowly lowered into the burial plot. The sound of rain drops on the lid of the casket would be their requiem. The man turned away from the woman to sleep.

"So...how does this make you feel?"

ABOUT
THE
AUTHORS

Niko Sonnberger is 60% H2O, 40% filmmaker who is putting the "try" back into "poetry".

Kris Kidd is a poet and essayist based in Los Angeles. He is the author of *I Can't Feel My Face* and *Down For Whatever*.

Dan Reilly is a multimedia artist and oyster shucker who used to write porno movies in Los Angeles, but now he makes magic in Brooklyn. He can be found on the internet @danohreally.

Caroline Bell is an American journalist, novelist, script and song writer. She is best known for her work in the field of medical advancement journalism, and has worked consulting or directly translating her work in that field to television. She has had several musical projects, including her current band *Bone Acre*, who play throughout Southern California. Her first novel, *Under Darkness* was optioned upon release, and she has two other novels currently in the works. She lives in Joshua Tree, CA with her partner and their dog.

Christopher Zeischegg is a writer, musician, and filmmaker who spent eight years working in the adult film industry as performer, Danny Wylde. He's the author of two novels, *Come To My Brother* and *The Wolves That Live In Skin And Space*, and the upcoming short story collection, *Body To Job*. Zeischegg lives in Los Angeles with his two cats, Victoria and Isis.

Ariel Rosenberg a.k.a. Ariel Pink enjoys reading, playing music, watching movies, eating, and teaching astronomy. He lives by himself in an apartment unit just above and behind Terra Mia coffee shop in the heart of Highland Park, CA.

Evan

Ingrid

Johnny

Caitlin

Stacey

Rachel

Rachel Plotkin is a writer living in Los Angeles who feels like she should be farther along by now. She struggles with work-life-love balance, and carries the inherent existential misery of being a Millenial from the Midwest. Her ex-boyfriend took this photo and sent it to her after the breakup once he had it developed.

Evan Sinclair is a television writer, living and working in Los Angeles. He lives with his wife, Aimee, and his two cats, Bear and Milky. His wife and his cats are not perfect, but they are perfect to him.

When she's not writing, **Ingrid Mouth** makes pornography and draws cool pictures. Email IngridMouth@gmail.com if you're a philanthropist looking to fund her sterilization.

Caitlin Dee is a singer and writer based in Los Angeles. Her husband is dead but is survived by two feral cats.

Stacey Beretta is a public figure/entertainer based out of Hollywood, CA. Recognized mostly as the front man for the band *Sons Of The Bitch,* he is known for his social satire and outrageous live performances. The self-proclaimed "Hollywood Outlaw" is currently working on a collection of memoirs from his time spent in Hollywood. The short story "New Years Eve" is his first published work.

Johnny Love rose to notoriety in the early 2000's as an enfant terrible of the Chicago DIY scene. After having his last space busted by the cops and having to escape to L.A. to avoid arrest, he was discovered by Daft Punk's manager and toured the world fueling his sex addiction and self-destructive behavior under the guise of playing music across four continents. He "retired" from dance music after the rise of EDM and the takeover of bro culture, and has recently gained notoriety as the creator of internet buzz subculture *Healthgoth.* He's currently spending his days staring at butts and making people do things that leave them sore for days while being paid for the privilege of doing so. He also really fucking loves cheesecake.

MJ

Dan

Chad

Damiano

Oriana

Dan Pederson is a writer. He likes to look at trees but doesn't tend to climb them. He lives in Minneapolis.

Damiano Villalobos is not an archetype by any design, but an enigma, birthed and molded in Los Angeles, searching for the faint glimmers of civilization left in this wicked, barbarous jungle that was one known as humanity.

MJ Brotherton is an artist living and working in Los Angeles. As a video/performance artist with an interdisciplinary background, their work revolves around their research and experiences in French eroticism, postmodern theory, illness, sex work, pornography, pharma-corporate America and millenial constructs of sexuality, gender, and media consumption/integration. Dead inside, they mostly do vicious and vile things behind closed doors with their feline sons and nasty hard drives.

Oriana Small a.k.a. Ashley Blue is an American author and pornographic actress. Her book, *Girlvert: A Porno Memoir* (Barnacle Books) is a best selling cult classic. She currently sells paintings and writes for *AVN Magazine* while residing with her husband, Dave Naz, and their cat in Los Angeles. You can keep up with her work at OrianaSmall.com.

Chad Fjerstad is an author responsible for two fictional works, *Popping Cherries* and *Warship Satan*. He operates the small multimedia production house *Ephemerol Night Terrors*, makes music videos, and plays in several Los Angeles-based music projects such as *Chiildren, Ass Life, More Ephemerol,* and *The Primals*. Chad also performs in adult films. His atypical perspectives tend to get him into occasional trouble.

EPHEMEROL
=NIGHT=
TERRORS

Printed in Great Britain
by Amazon